THE GREAT-GALACTIC
DANCE
COMPETITION
TRYOUT

K.B. LACEY

Text copyright © 2023 by K.B. Lacey
First Edition

Paperback: ISBN 978-1-912494-52-1
eBook: ISBN 978-1-912494-53-8

Edited by
Ali Jones, Ali Jones Studio / Kimberly Morgan / Diane Tassone

Character & Cover Background art by Amina Yaqoob
Book design by GetCovers

Published by:
Book Bubble Press
www.bookbubblepress.com

For my Abigail

The brilliant brain behind this concept.
Thank you for always being the quiet voice of reason.

ACKNOWLEDGEMENTS

It may take a village to raise a child, but it takes an army to raise an author. From production to marketing to a good cry on a shoulder, I have been blessed with support.

Meagan, Abigail and Neil, your love and support through this process has been undying even when I bored you to tears – you listened and that was all I needed.

I belong to a local Facebook mom group that when I reached out for help, hundreds – and I mean – hundreds of hands reached back. I was completely overwhelmed, and I don't think any of them truly know how much it affected me. OMC members – THANK YOU!

Being an author, living in imaginary worlds while trying to create a real-life emotions for readers can be very lonely. I would get tangled up in concepts, approaches, characters and sometimes get in my own way. If it wasn't for these people listening to my rollercoaster of emotions and championing me to keep going, I think I may have given up a while ago. Thank you, Margaret, Trevor and Eloise.

Mom, Dad and Ali, thank you for believing in me.

For anyone I did not mention, please know I am grateful.

I have the best author army!

FREE! STUFF

THE GREAT-GALACTIC

DANCE COMPETITION

VIP BOOK CLUB

✔ Parent Resources. Colouring Sheets, Crosswords, Puzzles.
✔ Bonus Scenes. Extra scenes not found in any books.
✔ Advanced Previews. Even new material before release!
www.kblaceyauthor.com

Dear Future Me,

Age: 6750 Years Old

I stayed up last night to find planet Jond Thab between the stars. It's a small planet somewhere up there, past the Gad Nor Sequence Star System. It's where all the greatest dancers

are right at this very moment, waiting to shine their brightest. It's where I will be someday.

SIGH

One day, I will look back out at those stars and wonder if someone like me is out there wondering the same thing.

I want this gigantic monster of a dream more than my live-beat adapter can measure. Sometimes it scares me how badly I want it.

If I close my eyes and concentrate, I feel my shoes on the floor of that big stage. Is that weird?

The problem is, I am not that good of a dancer. I am probably not GGDC - The Great-Galactic Dance Competition material. I shouldn't even be hoping to be on that stage.

SIGH

I am having a hard time getting my positions straight and my chordals tight like they are supposed to be. I look at people like Degmo, my best friend, and he makes it look easy. I hate that it makes me mad at him. It's not *his* fault, but why does it have to be so hard *for me*? I just don't understand it.

I want it more than he does, but my body refuses to cooperate! Yesterday in class, we did a stretching exercise to help us get more oxygen into our muscles so they can adapt to atmospheric tilts.
I stood up just like everyone else.
I stretched my arms out like everyone else.
I lifted my leg like everyone else.
Everyone else stayed there, still like statues, for five minutes.
Me?
I held that position for 3 seconds before I wobbled and fell.
No one looked at me, although I could swear I heard a muffled

laugh. I wished the floor would have opened up and swallowed me away.

It's not like I don't try. I do, I *really* do. I am sure that I do. Miss Ram-Y says I need to practice more and focus on my OPE rates — Oxygen Polynomial Exchange rates.

I make the adjustments, but it never works. I've checked and rechecked my calibration ratios and run a zillion diagnostic. I just can't do it! Werlo Cuz, my arch enemy, Miss Brightest-Start-In-The-Whole-Galaxy, said she could help me, and it took all my willpower not to stick my tongue out at her. If she asks me again, I'll step on her foot!

Yesterday I watched the GGDC semi-finals with Degmo. Mi-Ly, Ruk-9 and Carl Boles were competing. Mi-Ly was leading in points and a much better competitor than Ruk-9 and definitely better than Carl Boles, but during her performance she did a side-split-jump and landed on her ankle. It shattered.

Owwwch

Technicians flew to the scene to fix her. Degmo nudged me and said, "You know, she reminds me of you. I squinted, wondering

3

what was stirring around in his crazy mind. I shrugged like it didn't matter, but secretly I wanted it to be true.

Mi-Ly is the most talented dancer in the galactic-verse right now. She wins all the elements in her category, and as if that weren't enough, she is also pretty, with brown wavy hair, blue eyes, and one of the biggest cosmic ray smiles in all the galaxies.

I wondered what Degmo *really* meant. He's my best friend, but he could be a mean crater.

Did he mean I am like her because I am clumsy?

I threw a pillow at him just to be sure and he fake winced at the impact. He was about to launch it back when we were interrupted by what we saw and heard.

The medical technicians were carrying Mi-Ly off the stage while she howled through tears of pain or tears of anger. It was hard to tell, as both could apply. I felt bad for her. The finals were postponed until tomorrow. Then we'll find out what

4

happened to Mi-Ly, if she will continue to compete, or if it will be Ruk-9 and Carl Boles in the finals.

Next year is the big year.

This is the last year to make my future dreams come true. I will need to study the scientific publications for OPE variances so I can derive the correct calculations to neutralize my OPE Rates. It's the only way I can maintain atmospheric equilibrium and hold a tilt for a lot longer than 3 seconds!

???!!!

I do not know, but I will have to come up with a plan real soon and then the Great-Galactic Dance stage will be mine.

For as long as I can remember, I watched every Great-Galactic Dance Competition, no matter the planet, galaxy, or broadcasting schedule. Go ahead, ask me - ask me which planets have the best dancers.

Well, it's Xult from Fow Pac. She is the leading dancer - fast and light as a feather.

Best chordal shift is Kale Arno from Parch. He comes up with insane gravity-defying swings.

Best styles, I would have to say Umi Nor, or K-Sed. Both planets assimilate their planetary ecosystems into their costumes, which create amazing compositions.

WHOA

Let me slow down and introduce myself. My name is Fevah Seren. I am 7500 years old, and I am a walking library quarzone for things related to the GGDC - The Great-Galactic Dance Competition.

If you want to know anything about the vanguard competitors, up-and-coming dancers, or legacy competitors, experienced but not yet retired dancers, I know their names. I even know who should have won and why they didn't, based on *my* expertise, of course. Point distribution and technical rulings look no further than your friendly library quarzone dancer — me!

Which is why I want — with every synaptic spark of my capacitors — to compete at the next Great-Galactic Dance Competition.

Getting there will require some effort.

I must do these two-things:

1. Qualify for the L-Hite Dance Squad.

2. Convince Miss Ram-Y, my Principal Dance Director, to send us to the competition.

And by *us*, I mean *me*.

I'll worry about the convincing part later. Right now, I have to focus on the L-Hite Tryouts, which are open for younglings 7500 years or older, and I turned it 3 moons ago.

The L-Hite Dance Squad is a specialized group of high voltage dancers whose skills are perfected to represent my planet in dance competitions across the galactic-verse.

L-Hite Dancers are usually about 9500 years and older and at Level 2 or 3 Class Placements. Very few students from my class placement ever qualify, only one in the last 25000 years, in fact, and they made it all the way to the GGDC.

Like I said, I am a walking library quarzone.

Even though the chances of making it onto the squad seem like one hundred thousand millennia to one at my age - I may be slightly exaggerating - we are still allowed to try out. It's supposed to help bridge the hard work expected of us in the next Level 1, according to our teachers.

BLAH - BLAH

The loophole is that if you still have a few years at school in Above Quarter 4 — like me — then making it onto the squad rockets you to Level 1 without having to do the class work that comes with it.

More on that a bit later.

Now for the deets on my planet.

I live on a planet called Echo Rise, which is a fantastical and fearsome planet in the Gad Nor Sequence Galaxy Star System. I live here with my mom, dad, and younger sister, Luleh. Echo Rise is difficult to spot in the sky from Earth. If you hold 3 fingers up to the right of your moon —

BAM!

It's SO not right there!

Oh, my ode's song, gotcha!

You would need a mega-telescope to see me, but don't worry about that. I'll be doing that in person soon enough.

On Echo Rise, I live in Vector RonHeb, which is about 9000 light-miles from where I go to school in Vector Yergen. Most of my friends live in Yergen. They aren't very close, so I use a nub craft to move between them. A nub craft is slow and boring, and it stops everywhere to pick up passengers, but it's the only way I can get around. I could use a goop, like my parents, but I am not old enough to vault between vectors. I can't wait to be 12000 years old!

I call Echo Rise fantastical because we have two suns, two moons and two Change Tides seasons. Change Tides split the year into temperature intervals. Half the year, the sky is brilliant blues and dark purples. The other half of the year it shifts to brilliant oranges and pinks. It is hotter in Change Tide 2, and this is why the trees turn orange. It is also the Change Tide when we watch the colour waves as they make different shapes in the sky, such as rosettas and heel pants.

Some tourists say that my planet Echo Rise is too hot - they puddle and ooze, and it's all so very gross, if you can imagine.

YUCK

In fact, a few hundred years ago, a family of Earthers moved to Echo Rise and brought an air conditioner. The machine cooled the inside of their quarzone by breathing in air from the outside. It didn't work because the machine melted.

They moved back to Earth quickly after that. The whole reason they moved here in the first place was for their daughter to go to our school and learn how to be the best dancer in the galactic-verse.

We are the best. It's a galactic fact. We are faster than the speed of light and lighter than the gamma rays of our suns.

Echo Rise belongs to a string of planets that couldn't be more different from each other. K-Sed, the planet of the rich and fabulous, and Riach, the planet of the grey and dull. Their cloaks are grey, their hair is grey, and their food is grey.

BLAH

K-Sed is very cool and not just because of the climate. We go to K-Sed during Change Tide 2 because it is cooler. If you live on a hot planet, you go there for a break, in fact, most planets vacation there since a moon shades and cools half the planet. The antipodal point — the other side of the planet — is green, blue and yellow, with loads and loads of flowering trees. When I am famous, I'll be holidaying there too!

Now about my school…

I go to *Ram-Y Dance Academy*. It is the smartest and strongest school in the Gad Nor Sequences. We never lose a dance competition. Well, almost never. The moment planetary competitors see the L-Hite

Dance Squad arrive - they flinch. Our competitors know they've lost even before they've walked onto the stage.

Like I said earlier, I am in the Above Quarter 4 placement. My next placement is Entry Level 1, but it wouldn't be for many more years. Moving to Entry Level 1 comes with a LOT more noise.

Homework. Studying. Exams.

This is not thrilling, but it's what that placement offers that sweetens the deal. When you are in Entry Level 1, you have a much better chance of making it onto the L-Hite Dance Squad, although it's not a guarantee.

Becoming a member of the Squad will make the bestest — a most awesome — dream come true. Well, at least the start of it.

At Ram-Y Dance Academy, we learn the same subjects as other planets like *Languages*, *Astrophysics*, *History*, and *Math*. But on Echo Rise, we have two subjects other planets do not have — *Linearology* and *Dance*.

14

Linearology can be pretty tough to understand, but it's important for us. It teaches us how to move, bend, or arch our body to carry out a tonal skip, jump, or pivot. It helps us to adjust our dance routines to the gravitational conditions or atmospheric tilts of other planets.

I like Languages and Math, even though they aren't helping me with my OPE rates and calculations. History, I don't know... I just can't keep my eyes open when my teacher, Mr. O-Yer, starts talking about ancestors and planetary median triennial discoveries.

I can go on and on about my life on Echo Rise, but I must tell you one more thing which has been a solar burst in my side. I have a part-time job trimming the blind pikes at the Siew Home for Traditionals. All younglings have jobs that contribute to the planetary upkeep.

The job isn't the problem, it's what happened there that caused a celestial waterfall. The Siew Home is what Earthers call a retirement home for the elderly, and the planet Effendi calls Inc Etna for Amblers. However, here on Echo Rise, it's where our Traditionals live.

Traditionals build our living habitats like luxury quardomes for celebrities, multi-level capitol pods with 50 or more decks where people work like my mom and dad, or liveable quarzones like where I live in Vector RonHeb.

Traditionals take care of where we live, and I take care of the rear grounds outside their Home. I mow the blind pikes that grow like crazy, especially during Change Tide 1.

The Siew Home is surrounded by them. If you don't trim them quick enough, they cage you in and oh, my ode's song, the Traditionals really dislike that! The problem with blind pikes is as they grow, they become more solid and difficult to shave or break. When they are left unattended, they ruin the baseland, and our ground-level plain, becomes unliveable. Many Traditionals are over 45000 years old, and they hate to waste anything.

A few months ago, during Change Tide 1, my co-worker Blate attended a Dance Competition on Rodor which is in the Locus Galaxy. While she was away, the blind pikes grew too quickly and blocked the main entrance to the building! They summoned her back and then dismissed her. This upset her so much that she didn't even try to go back to the Rodor to complete the competition and missed the qualifying round. She wants to get her job back, but they won't even meet with her, and I am watching as those blind pikes grow and grow. It's a matter of time before they ask me to do it.

The front! Oh, my ode's song!

However, celebrating the glory and ambitions of my job came to a screeching halt the day before the L-Hite Dance Squad Tryouts.

The blind pikes at the Siew Home were long, and I was mowing them when a pebble flew off, destroying an oxygen switch from the inhalation port attached to the respiratory circuit board of my shell suit. The action caused a false reading on the generators and reversed my O2 exchange ducts. In other words, I breathed in too much dust and got an infection.

Dear Future Me,

Age: 4500 Years Old

Did you see that? WAIT!
I think I missed a position.
Let me show you again.
OH, MY ODE'S SONG, it's not working!

GRRR

I am just going to shut this off for a
bit.

...

I'm back!
It's the Neptune hurl, right?

I saw Xult do it at her last performance and the audience went
WILD!

Future self, make sure you look it up in the archives when you
put together the dance choreo for your L-Hite Tryout.

Miss Ram-Y will be like "Fevah, hmmm, this is the best
performance I've seen in a zillion years."

And I'll be like, "Thank you, Miss Ram-Y. I am the best. After all, you shouldn't expect anything less."

And she'll be like, "Of course, your Councillorship-madam, hmmm, I am your servant. My skills are your skills."

Imagine if she said that!

Imagine if she said I am the best!

Imagine if I am the best, then I'd be going to the GGDC, and everyone would be like FEVAH! FEVAH! FEVAH!

COUGH

"Fevah, what're you doing?"

Hey, Degmo, I didn't hear you get here. I am leaving a message for my Future Self, so I remember to do stuff when I am older.

"It's about to start. Hurry."

The Great-Galactic Dance Competition is on planet Yu Tu Na this year. My parents are saying it's a tiny landmass and that there are more competitors than resident lifeforms. The local Yu Tu Na competitor is Do TR A. There's a rumour that he can win it all this year and everyone across the galactic-verse is nervous. Xult doesn't seem like someone who gets nervous, but according to the News Sentinels, she is nervous *and* furious. Now *that* I can imagine.

Oh, my ode's song, it is going to be so exciting!

COUGH

Um, did I mention I am sick? It's Change Tide 2, and it's too hot this year. I got stuck in a sandstorm and it ruined my O2 exchange motherboard. It's SO frustrating because all I want to do is go outside and play with my friends, but my mom won't let me. That's another reason Degmo came over. I am getting so bored.

The doctors at Med Bay told me I have to wait a few more days. What's even worse than not being able to play, is not being able to dance. Anything like that would cause my chemical regulator to override and I would probably stop breathing which would be a bad thing. I know it is serious, but it is so BORING!

How am I supposed to get ready for GGDC when I can't do any of the choreos?

COUGH

"Fevah, are you dancing again?"

My mom.

GRRR

NO!

"You are coughing."

Oh.

"She knows. She heard you clopping."

Degmo, shhh!

How am I supposed to be the best when I can't practice? Sure, I have another 2000 years...

"3000 actually."

Shut up, Degmo!

3000 years before it matters, but still. Every minute counts.

COUGH

But I guess I can wait a few more days.

Moooommm, my head hurts.

The crackle of my ducts kept me up all night. The next morning, my mom sent me to Medical Bay for a check-up. Medical Bay replaced my switches and ran a wand over my chest to disintegrate the blind pike clouds. I would need to return in 5 days for another treatment which would remove all the clouds. They also said I shouldn't do anything that would accelerate my breathing, or the remaining particulate clouds would speed up my OPE exchange rate and I would short circuit my motherboard.

With two moons and two suns, the air in the Gad Nor Sequences Galaxy is thick. We need an air exchange pack to help us breathe.

The exchange pack is built into the top front of our shell suits. There are switches, circuits and filters that move the good stuff around and the bad stuff out, but when one of those gets damaged, it's a pain in the moon's crater!

The thick air is another reason those pesky blind pikes grow so thick and heavy. When they get too long and get cut, they crumble and create a lot of dust and gravel. They also cause damage if you aren't careful, and I guess I wasn't because I am in Medical Bay getting some super bad messaging.

I would have welcomed Med Bays advice with a

YIPPEE

But not today.

Why not today? The L-Hite Dance Squad Tryouts are happening TOMORROW!

Oh, my ode's song, my life's over.

"But Doctor, I have a dance tryout."

"Oh, for the L-Hite Squad?" The doc pushed up his glasses and leaned into the beep-blipping monitor. "My daughter tried out for that too at your age, but she didn't make it. She had to wait for the next placement cycle." He pushed a few more buttons on the monitor, and then waved me out. "With a bit of rest, you'll be fine, heh!"

My next stop was Buca Long. They run diagnostics on our shell suits when there is a malfunction. I hated going to Buca Long. The technicians always sounded suspicious, like *I* did something wrong.

I checked my comni while waiting for my suit diagnostics to complete. Comnis do a millennium of stuff like monitor our biometrics, measure our breathing cycles, and manage lighting contrasts, maps, and transfer credits.

Comnis are also our communication devices that connect us to each other. We attach comnis to our shell suits, but when we are not in them, we carry a small portable one that attaches to our wrists and right now it is blowing up—there were 17 messages!

```
> Did you sign up?
> Do you think you'll make it?
```

27

```
> Do you think I'll make it?
> It's finally here!
> ...
```

Degmo, my bestest-of-best friends, was trying to contact me. I told him this morning that I was going to Medical Bay, but he can be so forgetful sometimes.

I've known Degmo since birth. This sometimes seems too long when we are in a disagreement, but most of the time, it's great. We have a one-link channel on our comnis, so we talk all the time.

Degmo is the smartest student in my class placement and everyone — including me — thinks he'll make it onto the H-Lite Dance Squad on his first try, even though he doesn't think so. I — being his best, most loyal, honest friend — tell him he's terrible and nothing compared to my talents.

When Degmo is not strategizing about the GGDC, he's quantum gaming with lifeforms from other galactic-verses. He learns some interesting things, like there is a bird that tells you about your future on planet Alpha-Bor or that there is a star cluster that sings lullabies on planet Venus. He gets so involved in these adventures, which is why he can be forgetful. This was *not* the time to get forgetful, though.

Not only did it seem like a dark grey Riach cloud was following me around from being sick, but I also didn't have a way to communicate with him right now, and it was torture.

My version of the portable comni only receives incoming communications. I *need* an upgrade. I've asked and asked for a newer model, which has all the updates, and my mom keeps telling me, "We'll see." I am not hopeful for her to *see* it happening soon.

I needed to speak to Degmo ASAP. I eyeballed the CCC — the Courtesy Comni Controller was for emergencies only. Was this an emergency?

I waited for two minutes.
Two people left.
I got up and walked around.
I waited another two minutes.
Then the last person left.
No one was here, apart from the Buca Long technicians, and they

were in the back of the quarzone.

I flew to the dock and attached my sad portable comni to open my one-link channel with Degmo.

"FEVAH! Where are you? Miss Ram-Y released the tryout forms for the L-Hite Dance Squad."

"I am still at the digs in Buco, Deg, so keep it down!"

"When will you be done? You need to sign up." Degmo put on his best Miss Ram-Y voice and continued. I watched as Degmo stood with his hand tipped up in the air, imitating her posture. "If you don't sign up, hmmm, don't bother." I burst out laughing at the impersonation and my hands flew to my mouth to muffle the sound immediately.

A technician came out holding up a bright red and gold shell suit. His nose twitched when he saw my connection to the CCC.

"Is this yours?" he asked and gave me a look that dripped with disapproval.

 30

"Deg, I gotta go." I grabbed my suit and excused myself to a room. I reattached my device and pressed a credit transfer for the work done. Then I flew out of the Buco Long before the technician could read me the instructions for use of the emergency comni.

I was wondering if I should tell Degmo about not being able to try out for the L-Hite Dance Squad. Something inside flipped upside down. I didn't want him to feel bad for me. Plus, I just wanted to be left alone right now.

We'd been planning for this since we were 2250 years old. That's ALL we talked about. I kicked a rock and it sort of made me feel better.

GRRR, blind pikes!

I decided I should tell Miss Ram-Y as soon as possible and took a nub craft over to the Ram-Y Dance Academy.

I found Miss Ram-Y in her office hovering at the top row of her reading shelf. Miss Ram-Y wears a gravitational hydraulic boot. The boot gives her the ability to move quickly between and around classrooms and practice halls at the Academy.

31

I told her I would be able to attend the L-Hite Dance Squad Tryouts because the blind pikes had made me sick. Without looking up, she asked, "Did they spit a viral infection on you, hmmm? How did they make you sick, Fevah?" I rolled my eyes.

Inwardly, of course. Are you kidding? I wouldn't be telling this story if she had seen it!

I explained what I had done and how it had occurred. She nodded and arched her brow, asking for an event log for these visits.

A visit to Miss Ram-Y's office was an entertaining event. It's an enormous and awkward office. Papers and magazines overflowed from desks and shelves. Computers and pod connectors lay across the floor. Suits and costumes were tossed or piled on top of each other. One of her office walls had a mirror from top to bottom. This, in fact, made the office look worse because it reflected everything and looked a millennial light-year messier.

Miss Ram-Y, herself, is the complete opposite. She is organized and very neat. She knew everyone's name in the school along with their strengths and extreme detail on their weaknesses. It was not uncommon for her to walk by and ask, "Fevah, hmmm, how is your atmospheric tilt? Are you able to move to 37 degrees or are you still at 33.5 degrees?"

Her attention to detail also carried over to her neat appearance. She had long hair that was clasped tightly behind her head. It was as if her hair was imprisoned in that holder. She wore dark shells but often added a red or orange belt.

Miss Ram-Y was, in fact, shorter than me. She was shorter than most students, but she hovered over us. Sure, her gravi boots helped, but it was the way she stood. It was straight and long, like a moonbeam.

The Honour Wall drew my attention away from the hovering Miss Ram-Y. In contrast to the room's chaos, the Honour Wall was neat and organized, like Miss Ram-Y, and it held me spellbound. The wall was a buffet of medals, ribbons, and saved visual performances from all over the galaxies.

Like I said earlier, we win a lot, and all our awards and trophies found their home on this wall.

The Umi Trophy, a large obsidian cone with names of the winning team etched in gold, from the Berm Ked Solar System leaned against the wall. The heavy Lasa Gul Medallion from Elm Fury hung by a rod because it couldn't be worn by any dancer.

There were also costumes from Consort Dhoti which had an oily multi colour refractable hue and super cute pointed wooden clop hops from Ran Bred. The Jaray Nu Award from Pluto is a flat circular disc balanced on a glass triangle. I heard that the competition was tough, and we won on micro-points. But we won because we always do. We are the L-Hite Dance Squad.

There is one unusual part of the display, though. It is a large empty area with a small piece of paper that read:

The Great-Galactic Dance Competition trophy is called *The One,* since it is an individual trophy. Planets only sent the best to compete. Only one representative from each planet competes. The One is a diamond-blasted, silver-encrusted prehistoric earth sea siren that remains just out of grasp.

Nope, we've never won *that* one.

Ag Nu, a GGDC dancer who was the runner-up 998 years ago, called *The One* a nuisance. She was quoted as saying, "The One is like a splinter in your thumb you can't remove. It's a nuisance, yet we come here year after year to adore the beautiful lady." Ag Nu was an amazing dancer and should have won that year, but she lost on a misaligned Slip Whisper Pointe roll.

There is a rumour that Riach, our neighbouring grey dismal planet in the Gad Nors, put a curse on us with their toxic jealousy. We rarely see them at any competition and if we do, they never place. Riach dancers, I hear, are terrible. They move around like they are weighed down by the grey silver they wear. They remain characteristically sombre.

The One slipped away from us 17000 years ago. I know I said I am a library quarzone for all things GGDC, but this data point is difficult even for me. There is very little intel about this expedition, so I dismiss it as an old Traditional story.

This is why I was standing in her office today. I want to blast away the curses and re-imagine our reality.

The Galaxies needed to know Fevah Seren.

The hiss of Miss Ram-Y's gravitation hydraulics decompressing as she floated back down to the ground interrupted my gaze.

"Fevah, I asked you a question, and if the answer is satisfactory, I may reconsider, hmmm." Miss Ram-Y said.

I flipped open my comni, and searched through activities, then diagnostic logs and messaged her the log from my Medical Bay visit and Buco Long diagnostics for my suit.

She reviewed the logs and nodded. "Well, hmmm, it all seems in order. I'll add your name to my tryout list, Miss Seren."

Before I could respond, she flipped the gravi hydraulics on again and wafted back up. I couldn't help but wonder what she was reading, what was so interesting that she needed to go back. If she's a dance teacher, shouldn't she be working on dance choreography? I don't get teachers.

"But, but I won't be there. The doctor at the Med Bay said I had to wait five days before my OPE's equalizes," I said.

Miss Ram-Y didn't respond, and so I repeated myself, but louder this time.

"Good heavens, Fevah, hmmm, I can hear you. I was thinking. After the first tryout, I will shortlist several candidates for an additional performance. You may join that lot. It will be 5 days after the general tryout. That should give you plenty of time for your post-flux O2s to stabilize. Will that be alright with you, hmmm?"

I couldn't say yes. I couldn't say no. I couldn't speak. I was staring into the face of a golden privilege, and I couldn't find the words to respond.

So I stood there and stared at her trying to sort out what to do next.

"Anything else, Fevah, hmmm?"

"Why?"

Why?! Why?!

I couldn't just say *Thank you, Miss Ram-Y* and leave, no, I had to keep this going.

"Well, Fevah, dear, hmmm, talent is a celestial gift, I want to use it for our advantage."

Before she turned and disappeared behind a shelf, she said, "And

Fevah dear, hmmm, please be careful around those blind pikes." I left her office lighter than any gravitational hydraulic release.

Dear Future, Fevah,

Age: 750 Years Old

Happy 750th Birthday, my spinning neutron star.

I wanted to call you Pulsar, but your dad thought it sounded like a vegetable. He wanted to call you Quasar, which is equally bad. Luckily, we both could agree on Fevah, and I think it fits you more and more each day.

Anyway, you are probably wondering why I am sending you this message from the past. Well, it is for an excellent reason. Last night, I had a wonderful dream about you.

You were taking a trip to a faraway planet. You were much, much older, maybe 15000 years old. Goodness, you were so beautiful and tall. You were nervous about your trip, but you didn't want to admit it. You held my finger, like you are doing now.

See, you are wrapping your entire hand around my finger.

We were at the airport waiting for your flight. It was loud and busy. Chaotic and just noisy. There were passengers everywhere talking and laughing, pushing about, or sleeping.

Transportation vehicles were zipping everywhere to pick up someone or something and then take off again. We held hands and watched it all go by. Goodness, we stayed there for hours, letting the room orbit around us.

The airport was broadcasting the Great-Galactic Dance Competition, and we moved to a lounge seater to watch it. I don't recall who was competing. I just remember watching it and feeling happy leaning up against you.

It felt... ummm... peaceful would be the word.

After a few hours, or it could have been a few minutes — it was a dream, it's hard to tell the time — someone called out, "There she is!" I sat upright to see whom they were talking about. Suddenly, we were surrounded by hundreds of lifeforms taking visuals and shouting your name. In the middle of that, you turned to me and said, "It's ok, mom. I got this."

The flashes were hurting my eyes, and I covered them. I called out to you, "Fevah, where are you?" but you didn't answer. I kept calling and calling, and I was getting scared.

FEVAH!

The next thing I remember is you tugging on my elbow. We are back at home, and you are 6000 years old. You leaned your head on my shoulder like you are doing now and asked, "Mom, will I make it?" I didn't answer your question because it felt really hard to, but I nodded.

I don't know if that dream means anything. It may not, but it happened the night before you were born. The dream seemed so real! I felt the orbital pain from the blinding lights and felt your hair on my cheek, from when your head was on my shoulder. I know it's crazy to laugh about it, but I don't see how it didn't happen. Something is telling me it is an important dream that is leading to something even more important.

I am taking an enormous leap, and I am recording this message to your future self for delivery on your 7500-year birthday. At 7500 years old, you can try out for the L-Hite Dance Squad.

Only one member of the dance squad can be sent to the Great-Galactic Dance Competition, and I am betting it will be you, even though we haven't sent anyone in thousands of years. You may think I am crazy when you receive this, and you wouldn't be wrong, but what if I am right?

Fevah, no matter what, I will always — ALWAYS — be your biggest fan, no matter what you or anyone thinks. We will not always get along, oh, my ode's song, we may even be in a disagreement when you receive this, but just remember that my love for you is bigger and brighter than any supernova. If I have forgotten how to dream this big by the time you receive this, please remind me! Love, Mom xo

Last night I had a strange dream. The type of dream that follows you into the morning and sabotages your day. The dream started with a News Strobes announcement through our Receptor Visions.

"A massive round of applause for Aubry Trewn from Planet Echo Rise in the Gad Nor Sequences. I am pleased to announce to the galactic-verse that this young lady won first place at the Great-Galactic Dance Competition. It is an honour for me to declare that magnificent people live beyond our stars."

The picture broadcast of Aubry Trewn was actually a picture of me. She had brown hair to her shoulders, with waves and curls that were being trampled by a small hair band. Blue eyes stared back at me, smiling and holding a bouquet. A microphone pushed its way through the crowd, and someone asked, "Aubry, Aubry, one question. How did you do it?"

I responded, "With a boomerang."

Everyone clapped, like that was exactly what I should be saying.

I was startled by a tug on my leg. When I looked down, a little girl asked for my autograph. The little girl also looked just like me, and I was annoyed. I shook my head and said, "Go away. This is embarrassing."

The girl pulled back into the crowd and vanished.

"There you have it, Ladies and Gentlemen, Organic Forms, and Micro Complexes. She won it all with a Boomerang."

The next moment I am on a goop, being hurled across the galaxies to get home. My sister caught up to me and asked where I was going. I pointed, "There!"

"Okay, but I will tell mom."

She stuck her tongue out at me, so I pushed her off the goop and she landed on a pile of blind pikes. An enormous cloud swelled up around her, and I coughed. My live-beat adapter made strange sounds.

Ba-Boom-Crack

When I opened the panel, small rock pebbles tumbled out into my hand. I wondered, what is this?

Then I heard the hiss of Miss Ram-Y gravitational hydraulic boots as she floated down in front of me and crossed my name off her tryout list. "I told you to be careful!"

A voice called my name, but I couldn't tell where it was coming from. It seemed to move every time I looked in that direction. The voice stopped as Degmo appeared beside me. "Fevah, you made it! I gave you those rocks for good luck. What do you think?"

The next thing I knew, I fell to Earth. A lullaby was playing, and my legs twitched. I felt ridiculous and sloppy as I moved into a dance position.

Keep going. Keep going, I whispered to myself.

I got up onto a large stage, and as I moved across it, my legs felt like blocks of lava rocks. I moved in a slow, absurd circle for hours. When the outlandish performance ended, I bowed to the audience, and as I stepped off the stage, I tripped.

The little version of me that pulled my leg for an autograph stuck her foot out.

"What did you do that for?!" I screamed.

She bent over and laughed. The audience roared with laughter.

My vision receptors connected to Echo Rise, and I saw more laughter - my parents, Degmo and Miss Ram-Y. The last thing I remembered was thinking, "I want to go home."

***

My alarm buzzed a few hours after first sunrise, but I stayed in bed, staring at the ceiling. I didn't want to get up. The dream was weighing me down. What could it mean?

I stumbled into the kitchen and triggered a series of events, causing a celestial waterfall of chaos. I bumped into a chair, then the counter. My elbow ploughed into a cup that spun around and collided with a glass filled with juice that spilled onto the counter.

My dad looked up. "What's up with you this morning? Didn't you get enough sleep? You need to turn off your one-link with Degmo. Talk to him at school." I rolled my eyes.

The commotion got my mother's attention. She came over and opened my diagnostic panel, looking for error codes. This was so annoying. I could do that myself. I wasn't 3000 years old anymore!

I didn't need a lecture right now. I figured I may as well come clean with a legit reason for my state. "I had a bad dream."

"Well, if it was bad, then it wasn't a dream. It would have been a nightmare." My dad said.

I rolled my eyes.

My mom wiped up the juice on the counter and glared at my dad. "Before we decide what it was, do you remember anything about it?" I nodded and told them what I could remember.

My dad made a face like he just ate a bitter, prickly plum. "Aubry Trewn? Haven't heard *that* name in a while." A chime interrupted us, and he picked up his bag. "Feel better, kiddo." He spoke into his comni saying that he'd be right there and left for work.

My mother came around the counter and sat down next to me at the table.

"It was just a bad dream, Fevah. You were sick, and your O2 generators weren't working. You may have had more damage than we thought." She said as she continued to fidget with the suit. "Maybe you should go back to the Medical Bay to make sure there wasn't any other damage." Her hands were working their way across my suit to the live-beat adapter pack, checking for loose connectors.

I told her about what Miss Ram-Y said about me trying out with a shortlist. My mom thought that was a great idea but also thought that I should wait and try out in a few years.

WHAT?! No Way!

This blew my mind because she *knew* how much it meant to me.

"Next time?! No way! I am going to GGDC." The words tumbled out of me before I could pull them back.

Mom sighed. "Fevah." I know what that meant, and I didn't want to hear it. Sure, we haven't sent anyone to the GGDC in thousands of years, but it doesn't mean that it could never happen. I want to be the one that would put Echo Rise back on the galactic map again, but I can't get anything right.

Everything was working against me.

I put down my spoon and pulled back my chair. The first sun meal was over.

If it was even possible, the day got even worse from there. At school, all classes were focused on the E-Lite Dance Squad Tryouts. Astrophysics focused on how the body creates angles and arcs based on analogical wave streams. History focused on the evolution of competitions and their importance in our social inter-relations with planets and co-patriot galaxies. Linearology reminded us of how balance and strength affected our O2 exchanges based on environmental conditions.

Then there was a Transitional Dance which was fun because we didn't do anything except stretch and listen to the quiet aural dopler wave sounds. It would have been the best class to block out the surrounding chao, but there was another of Miss Ram-Y's notes on the door.

Be of help
or let
help find you

I suppose that meant that if you were not trying out you were expected to support another student who was. If you are rehearsing for your tryout, then you should listen to any advice offered.

This meant that I had to either listen to someone complain about how nervous they were. Or worse, I would have to listen to someone who was too excited.

In both cases, I wished I could crawl into a moon crater and hide.

There was nowhere to go for any other type of distraction. The galactic-verse was against me. It was so not fair.

I wandered around looking for Degmo. When I found him, he was clearly in the *let help find you* group. Degmo was buzzing like a zyme. His excitement was plain to see as I walked up to him. He was playing with his gravitational hydraulics. He had a pair just like Miss Ram-Y, and although he didn't need them, if it was the newest model, then he would definitely have it.

"Hey, Degmo."

He waved a greeting without looking up. He was adjusting the controls on his boot. He turned it on and floated for two seconds, then turned it off, and a hiss brought him back down. He did those three more times. I watched him, very unimpressed.

Then he opened his O2 motherboard panel and changed his OPE rates. This incredibly ridiculous action paused his breath, causing him to sputter and cough. He readjusted his controls, stabilized, then waited a few seconds before doing it all over again only to get the same result. Before he tried for the third time, I interrupted this bizarre experiment and asked what he was doing. "I am practicing breathing on Earth."

Earth? Why Earth?

He read my mind, "Because that is where the Great-Galactic Dance Competition is being held this year, Miss-I-Know-Everything-About-The-GGDC! The air is thinner, and I want to start my breath training early."

Oh, my ode's song, I forgot!

Degmo laughed. "I am being forward-thinking and ready for any big announcement."

"What's up with you?" he asked when he noticed I wasn't laughing at his ridiculous antics.

"Nothing. Only that my life is over." I whined. What else was there to do? So, I told him.

Dear Future Me,

Age: 6000 Years Old

I am so BOOOOORED.

SIGH

Degmo has been on vacation for a gazillion years, and I have absolutely nothing to do.

Well, he's been gone since the start of summer vacation. His dad said that this year Change Tide 2 is too hot and that they needed to get some shade and cool down. So off they went to K-Sed to relax under their moon.

I asked my dad if we could go too, and he said we couldn't because his job needs him to stay here on Echo Rise. I told him he should get a job that didn't, so we don't melt this year, and he laughed.

CAN YOU BELIEVE THAT?!

He said I'll understand it someday. Well, someday could have been yesterday or today, and I still don't understand it. All I know is that I am so bored without my best friend.

Degmo is the best. He is smart, almost the smartest kid in Quarter 1 Placement. He always comes up with the best games when I get bored. But one of the craziest things about him is that he is so clumsy - clumsier than me, even, which makes me laugh all the time.

If there is a wall, he will walk into it. If there's a chair, he will knock it over. He's broken wrists, knees, and even his O2 exchange pack hundreds of times. He doesn't do it on purpose. He just gets distracted and forgets to look out for himself. I help him do that. I am always saying, "Deg, watch out!"

One reason he is so distracted is that he talks a lot. By a lot, I mean all the time. He always has a story or song or new choreo on his mind. It's great that he thinks about these things, but he also wants to tell everyone exactly what is on his mind. Most of the time, I enjoy listening because his thoughts are exciting to listen to, but sometimes it's like I am a pea trapped in a beanbag.

When I am sad — like I am now because he's not here — he knows exactly how to make me laugh. A few years ago, a Tensab, a large animal that lives in the greenie pods and only comes out at night, trampled my flower cube. I cried and cried.

Degmo painted his face pink and drew a big white smile. I laughed for days after that.

My dad has been trying to get me to laugh by telling me jokes that really aren't that funny, or maybe they would be if I was 37500 years old. My sister has been telling me an endless story about her colouring book that went missing, and that she thinks that Nellie the Otterbotter, a class animal, ate it. I am not exactly sure if she thinks it's true or not, and I really don't care. I just want Degmo to come back so we can hang out.

Next week, Rodor will host the Great-Galactic Dance Competitions. The days building up to the GGDC are about gathering intel on the competitors such as their strengths, weaknesses, points earned, or awards won in pre-comps and, finally, whom we predict is going to win.

After we analyze all the important stuff, we write our winner, place it in my giant trophy-shaped jar, and we wait. At the end of the Competition, whoever wrote the correct winner wouldn't have to do their homework for the first week of school. I've won the last 3 years.

Well, we started this tradition 3000 years ago, and so far, I'm the only champion. It's fortunate for Degmo. He doesn't want me to do his history homework, anyway.

We still talk every day through our one-link channel. His quardome on K-Sed is next door to a family from Riach. He tells me they only come out at night when it's dark. They are silver and grey lifeforms that reflect light. The daylight, even under a moon shadow, hurts their eyes, so they come out at night when it's easier to see.

Degmo won't be returning to Echo Rise for another three weeks. He'll miss my birthday tomorrow and I will have three weeks of complete and utter boredom.

SIGH

If I hear any more of my dad's jokes, I think I'll run away to Riach!

Degmo's parents are Sentinels. Sentinels oversee the news broadcasts that are watched through our Receptor Visions. You could say it's one way we gain knowledge. With that job, they have access to a lot of information. Their quarzone was literally a collection of micro nodes and data on both computers.

"Let's find a port where I can connect and tap into my parents' catalogues and look up this Aubry Trewn," Degmo said.

He plugged into a data bot. While we waited for initiation, he drummed his fingers deep in thought. "I kind of remember the name. She was a famous legacy dancer, I think."

That part was true, but that is all I knew of her as well.

Degmo typed in her name and waited.

    No results were found.

He changed his search parameters to search for legacy dancers. Many names were listed, but not hers.

    No results were found.

He continued his search by typing in various combinations of search strings.

    No results were found.

The checks were returning zero results, so we continued to the auxiliary media library and used those output connectors. The output connectors connected us to the galactic-verse of information and not just from Echo Rise. "Won't you get into trouble if your parents find out?" I said, scanning the room. I couldn't help but wonder if they were watching.

"No way! It's research. They love that stuff." Degmo chirped. He typed a few codes and shook his head some more. "Nothing... Hmmm. Let me try a reference indicator. Do you think she lives here or in another galaxy?"

I shrugged. "In my dream, it didn't feel like I was *here*." I circled my arms around me to mean standing here on this planet.

He hmmm'ed again, and I giggled because he sounded like Miss Ram-Y.

Degmo kept entering codes — singular and binary algorithm searches until...

"THERE! I found her!" Degmo read the reference in the news strobe while I hovered behind his shoulder.

"Oh, interesting," Degmo nodded a few more times, and his eyes grew wide again as he projected the story and read it out loud.

Aubry Trewn was an advanced dance composer. She didn't just choreograph dances, she created them through her advanced study of Linearology and Interstellar Physics. One of her infamous dance moves is the Trewn Tip Pirou, which is a blend of ancestral ballet and vintage hip hop.

That was it!

That was why her name sounded familiar. The Trewn Tip Pirou. We learned about that in Linearology, but it's an advanced movement for Entry Level 1 students.

The Trewn Tip Pirou was first unveiled on Elm Fury, where Aubry received the Usa Gut Medallion. The competition was fierce, but the Trewn Tip Pirou tipped the scales into Echo Rise's favour through nano points. Aubry has kept our beloved planet on the galactic map, and we are proud to have her as one of our own. Let's not forget her equally stellar mentor Ram-Y Nivelles, who Aubry proclaims was her inspiration.

"That's Miss Ram-Y!" I exclaimed. Degmo shushed me and continued.

Aubry qualified for The Great-Galactic Dance Competition, but an extraordinary mishap prevented that from happening. In a backstage practice session, Aubry's capacitors had blown a fuse and overrode her breathing lines. As you all know, this causes an

ignitable fume between the bindings of suits. She
was…

"Dead?" I whispered.

"No! Unconscious. Not moving."

The Medical Techs worked on her and reversed some of
the damage, but she would never dance again. She left
Echo Rise 18000 years ago. Destination unknown.

Was that why it was so hard to find information about her?

Was she banished because she failed?

Where is she now?

Does she miss home?

The questions swirled around me but didn't seem to bother Degmo.
He shrugged and looked at the clock. "Time for me to go."

Degmo was getting ready for the L-Hite Dance Squad Tryout.

GRRR, blind pikes!

65

It was not fair!

I was worried.

What if Degmo qualifies for the team and I don't? My heart would totally and completely break.

What if I qualify for the team and he doesn't? Would his heart totally and completely break?

Degmo says I am the better dancer. Sometimes we pretend bad-dance-offs just to prove how awful we are. Those routines are so much fun, but usually end up with him falling or bumping into something that requires a visit to Medical Bay.

There is no way that Degmo wouldn't make it onto Miss Ram-Y's short-list.

When someone makes it to the shortlist, they have one more chance to show off. They add more movement and more positions. They may speed up or slow down, but they have the time to make everything better. Would my dance choreo performance equal a short-list choreo?

 66

I didn't think there was an answer to this, and it made me extremely uncomfortable. I took a deep breath, and my live beat adapter blipped from the unbalanced oxygen intake.

I walked Degmo to the Dance Hall and wished him good luck.

"Let me know how it goes," I said. We gave each other our secret groove-shake, and he walked in.

What else was there for me to do except go home and wait?

It was just past the first moon, and I had just finished my homework when Degmo one-linked me. He said there were 18 dancers and Miss Ram-Y disqualified three of them for an incorrect wardrobe.

I gasped. "What were the infractions?"

Laces untied, hair was not pulled back, and a uniform infraction. "Fevah, you couldn't even see the rip. The cuff of the pant leg was frayed and had loose strings hanging outside of the boot."

GASP

I gasped again. I didn't know we were also being judged on a dress code.

Oh my ode's song.

I asked how he thought he did, and Degmo shrugged. He thought he did all right. He said he didn't really want to talk about it and was glad it was over. I guess I would feel the same way. So, I changed the topics to talk about the nominees for the next GGDC. He didn't want to talk about that either and said he'd see me at school tomorrow.

All night I lay awake wondering what had happened. Did he do well? Did he fall or trip? Did someone say something awful? Was he upset I wasn't there? Did he think talking about it would hurt my feelings? Was it even about me? Was he planetary supersonic and did so awesome that he didn't want to tell me? My stomach tightened, and I tossed and turned.

Tomorrow the first round of names will be announced, and I'll know then.

Patience. Patience. Patience.

This is something I don't have.

My legs were twitching as I mentally walked through my choreo.

Could I compete with them?

I am not sure how I would handle it if Degmo made the team, and I didn't. I know, without a doubt, I would be thrilled for him. He is my best friend and I want us to do this together, but right now I must leave it up to the interstellar fairies.

The second moon rose, and my mind went to where it shouldn't have let it go. I started imagining what I would say to if he made the L-Hite Dance Squad and I did not.

I would say, "I am so happy for you, Degmo. I knew you always would." That part would be true.

He'd say, "Thank you. You are an excellent dancer, too." That would upset me and I would think, *well, not good enough.*

What if I try out and look silly?

My comni buzzed, and Degmo's face popped up. I pressed connect, and he came to life. "Sorry about earlier, Fev. I was just nervous, I guess. You'll do so much better than any of us there today. I am 100% sure."

A rogue tear slipped down my cheek from relief, or fear, or a bit of both. "Thanks, Deg. Good night."

***

"Attention Dancers of Miss Ram-Y Dance Academy." Miss Ram-Y's voice booms through the school Comni System

"After careful review and consideration, the dancers who will progress to the next round are Werlo Cus, Nea Lenn, Poli Rocas, Erno Doog, Catio Recmo, Ider Cing, Orat Gemen, Gura Tonis, Offe Giner, and Degmo Sokz. Thank you, students, hmmm. In the next round, I will select five of my best dancers for the L-Hite Squad. I look forward to seeing what you will do with your talents, hmmm."

"Yes!" Degmo hooted and pumped the air. "We made it!"

"Deg, *you* made it. *I* still have to try out," I reminded him.

"True, but you're on the shortlist, so you are halfway there!"

"No, I didn't make it to the shortlist. I was sick, remember? I didn't try out the first time." I said he was forgetful, right?

"But it doesn't matter, Fev. You will make it. I know you will." He sauntered to the left. He stepped to the right, curved one arm above his head, and spun around while dipping to the floor into a low bow.

"Can't you just hear it?" Degmo stood back up and put his hands to his mouth, imitating the sound of an excited audience. Degmo's eyes lit up, and I truly doubt he saw anything but himself on stage, the Great-Galactic Stage, and my confidence tripped and sprawled across my ego.

Dear Future Me,

Age: 3750 Years Old

OMOS, I am so excited! I just won the role of Queen Candles.

We had tryouts yesterday, and today I got picked to perform at the Change Tide 1 Festival at the Siew Home.

I know, I know, Change Tide 1 is not for months, but it's a big production, so tryouts are over Change Tide 2, with practices starting even before school starts!

Me! OMOS!

Me, Degmo, Werlo and Orat won the roles. The performance is called 'The Dance of Fahrenheit.'

Like I said, I am the Queen of Candles.

Degmo is the Whispery Wind.

Werlo is the Clocktower. Werlo was upset she was this Queen and cried about just standing still.

Orat is an Aperture - something about an opening to a lens

that lets light pass through.

Orat is slow. Orat is slower than Nellie. If he is supposed to be a telescope, and if light moves fast, then we may all be there until the next Change Tide 1! But Mr. O-Yer, my history teacher, thought he was the best dancer for the performance.

Queen of Candles is the Queen of a Sun Kingdom that is having trouble getting rid of an angry element stirring up dust and dirt and blocking out the light. That's the Whispery Wind.

Degmo is kind of the bad guy. He's supposed to stop me from making the world a brighter place and push against the arms of the clock tower on the clock tower to stop time. We do a big dance-off, and he dies while Werlo, Orat and I celebrate.

My costume is so pretty, too. I can't wait to wear it! It's a long white dress which is shorter on the front so I can move and is long and drags on the ground behind me. I even get to wear a bright red and gold crown. I must pull my hands behind me so I look straight and tall. The reason I got this role is that I got the best grade in General 2 Linearology. I even beat Degmo, who is the best at everything.

Yippee! Oh, my ode's song, I am so excited!

Today is my birthday, and it is the best birthday present ever!

I am so excited. I knew I would get there. I spent every day since the last performance memorizing the choreo. I also made sure I studied extra hard for those Linearology tests. I had to get my dad to help me with them. The calcs with the circuitry adjustments can be pretty complicated. He knows a lot about that stuff. He told me to be patient and work out the numbers before jumping into the adjustments.

Patience? Me? Ha!

Yes, it was hard, but it was totally worth it. I am so excited that I feel like I am floating across the sky like a rosettas or heel pants. Soft and puffy. Oh, hey, they are also white. I am dressed in white! Everything is lining up perfectly today.

It's my birth-DAY. I am Queen of Cand-LES.

It's my birth-DAY. I am Queen of Cand-LES.

It's my birth-DAY. I am Queen of Cand-LES.

I have to go now. I just wanted to let my future self-know that I did it!

UPDATE!!!!!

I know this is off-schedule, but I had to add one thing. I just performed at the Siew Home, and they loved me. I had three standing ovations. The Traditionals posted a job opening for a youngling to cut the blind pikes in the backyard - I think I'll apply. I will win that, too. I am on a roll!!

Making it through the rest of the day was so retrograde. It was slow and moving in the opposite direction to how I felt. Everyone was hugging and laughing, and you would think that the mood would have been contagious, but it wasn't.

I was not happy. In fact, I wanted to kick cheeriness in the shins and then trample all over it.

When I was sick, I missed three days of work and the blind pikes needed to be trimmed. This time, I turned down my respirator, so the intake valve didn't pull in any dust.

A long mirror reflected a ray of sunlight and caught my eye as I was putting away the blind pike's cutter. I glanced around, wondering if anyone would notice if I walked closer to have a better look.

I made a face, and my reflection repeated it right back. I giggled, and this time exaggerated a fancy dance bow.

Then, from somewhere deep in my memory, I heard the song from my dream: "Raglan Chrome."

My legs and arms melted into the melody of the low and high frequencies.

I forgot about my chest infection.
I forgot about the rules.
I forgot about where I was.

My toe circled a patch on the floor as my left leg anchored to the ground. My arms swooped, my back elongated, and I moved in time with the music with as much grace and poise as a breeze through Change Tide 2.

When the music drifted away, I stopped and bowed, properly this time, to my reflection in the mirror; and that's when I received the applause.

I spun around to face three Traditionals clapping from a seat tucked away against the wall. They must have been there earlier, but I hadn't noticed them.

Oh, my ode's song, I'm in trouble. It'll be like Blate. They are going to fire me, and just before my try out. "I'm so sorry. I di-didn't know anyone was … Sorry," I stuttered and bolted to the door, but a shrill voice stopped me.

"Wait!" Their voices combined and amplified the command.

I retraced my steps back into the room. They are going to tell me I can't come back, that they are going to give my job to another, more responsible student. My live beat adapter slowed and alerted me to the sudden drop. I adjusted my vent and raised the OPE Rate.

"That was lovely, my dear. Could you do another one for us?" the same voice queried, but this time softer.

Just like Kuiper's Belt, a large ring of icy fear clasped at my throat, and my reply got stuck behind it. I shook my head.

"Well, that is a shame," the Traditional replied. "We don't get to leave our quardomes much anymore, and we miss watching our young talent. Once a year is not nearly enough." She chuckled and tilted her head to the side. "Are you one of Miss Ram-Y's students? You must be her favourite."

I shyly giggled and shook my head again.

"I am Midi, and my friends here are Flexis and Carest," Midi announced, tilting her head with a smile.

Carest and Flexis were deep in conversation and hadn't noticed the introduction. Flexis seemed stuck on her point. "It's her shoulder blades, not her knees. Look at them!" Flexis turned towards me, then Carest, and then turned back to continue with their discussion.

Awkward

Carest shook her head and disagreed, but Flexis continued, "If her shoulders are not pointed in the direction her body is moving, her frame will overcompensate with the centrifugal point, and she will have a negative offset." My eyes widened at the intensity of the technical breakdown.

Carest snorted. "You don't learn that until after Level 5, Flexis." Carest shushed her friend and turned to me. "What's your level, youngling?"

"Above Quarter 1," I whispered.

"Above Quarter 1!" they cried out in unison. Flexis was the tall one and held her height up straight like a ruler, like Miss Ram-Y. She bowed slightly, and her large side curls bounced. "Well... ahem... then, my dear, Carest has won this argument. I presumed you were older. Impressive technique for a youngling." With that, she turned to leave.

"I'm getting ready to try out for the L-Hite Squad, and I was... I was just practicing. I'm sorry for the interruption."

Flexis whirled back around, curls bobbing. "Does that mean you will represent us at the Great-Galactic Dance Competition?" she asked.

"It's in Umi Burn," Carest said.

"No, Neptune," Midi corrected and flicked her cape around her shoulders to end the conversation.

"Alpha Strait," Flexis insisted. Within moments, they were arguing about who knew more about the administration of the competition. I interrupted their debate. "It's on Earth this year. But we don't go to that competition anymore. I'm just trying to make it onto the L-Hite Squad," I added.

Carest, the smallest of the group, wore a silver shell suit with pink straps, and she looked like a youngling herself as she stepped forward and pirouetted. It looked just like a candle flicker.

Flexis muttered and rolled her eyes to the ceiling. "Here we go." Then added, "Show off!"

Midi stepped in front of Carest, and showed the Sauté Branig, which is a jump with a sweeping leg extension that started at Carest and stopped abruptly behind Flexis' heels.

Flexis continued to mutter. "You, too? Well, then…" Flexis took a few steps backwards to find more space and started with a slight scrape of her toe against the floor, like scraping a match to light, and just like that, before our eyes, Flexis shimmered. She continued with several rapid movements, and my jaw dropped. She was doing the Trewn Tip Pirou — Aubry Trewn's signature dance step. Carest and Midi laughed and clapped. "Yes, Flexis, yes!"

"And that, my fellow Traditionals, is how you properly show off to a youngling."

I was so bedazzled that it took me a few moments to find my words. "That was the Trewn Tip Pirou," I said.

"Goodness, she's a bright one, too," Flexis replied.

Carest was still beaming. "Flexis is the best at it... Well, the second best, I suppose."

"Do you know Aubry Trewn?" I asked.

"Well. Now. That is true." Flexis puffed and looked at her comni. "I've been moving too much. This crazy thing is telling me to adjust my metabolic exhaust levels."

Carest reached up to wrap her arms around Flexis' hips, ready to provide support. "Flexis don't do too much. Your height and age alone are enough to muddle up your chemistries. You'll be in Medical Bay, and our Project will be delayed."

Midi gave me another tilted smile and said, "It was a pleasure meeting you today, youngling. We had a wonderful time remembering. Please let us know how you did after your tryout. You'll give them the Neptune hurl."

"I am very nervous." I said the words before I thought them out. I hadn't planned on admitting that out loud to them or anyone.

Flexis tapped the side of her head as she leaned into Carest and advised, "**Pfff**! Say you'll do it, and you'll do it. Say you *think* you'll do it, and all you'll ever do is *pretend* that you can. Body and mind respond to *Dos,* not to *Thinks.* Remember that Miss-Above-Quarter-1."

***

That night I couldn't sleep. It wasn't another bad dream, but about my encounter with the Traditionals - Carest, Flexis and Midi. They thought I was good.

Was I?
Were they just being kind?
I wonder if I am as good as Aubry.
My confidence was rattled, and I didn't know how to put it back together.

The first round of try outs had resulted in tough competitors. I had to double my skill just to be equal to them. I didn't know if I could do that. If you had asked me last week before the blind pike's incident, I would have said

No Problem - Easy.

I will make the L-Hite Squad and then I will win the Great-Galactic Dance Competition.

The other dancers were amazing. I don't think I am anything compared to them. Even Degmo is incredibly skilled - like he already belonged on the L-Hite Dance Squad. I would look ridiculous trying to keep up with them.

I should withdraw.

I couldn't, though. Miss Ram-Y had given me an exception because I whined about being sick. For the hundredth time...

GRRR, blind pikes!

The Siew Home mirror felt like a magical portal filled with interstellar fairies.

Oh, my ode's song, it felt... it felt...

Electrifying!

That's the word. It was electrifying! My body moved without a glitch or a flinch. I wanted that moment to last forever. But my capacitors accelerated, and my live-beat adapter tha-thumped fast. I wanted this more than I dared hope, and it filled me with fear rather than filling me with ambition.

Maybe that is what Flexis meant. What was it she said again?

 86

Say you'll *do* it, and you'll *do* it. Say you *think* you'll do it, and all you'll ever do is *pretend* that you can.

I decided I was going to do.

Dear Future Me,   Age: 2250 Years Old

I wonder if there are younglings on other planets that feel invisible, too. Sometimes, no matter how hard I try, I feel like no one sees me or if they do; they want to fast-forward past me and move to the next thing because it is more exciting. I know I

am not interesting. I can't help that. Ok, I am getting leaky again. Let me tell you what happened.

A few weeks ago, at the end of Change Tide 1, I graduated from Entry Level 2. A few weeks from now, after the Change Tide 2 break, I will be in EL3 - Entry Level 3.

EL3 is hard, so we need to take a one-week crash class on Gravity to make sure we are ready for it. I hear EL3 is really dark matter, and that Miss Ram-Y looks for perfection.

Who wants to grow up and be Miss Perfect, anyway?

In Gravity Class, after the second sun break, we do stretches and jumps, which we call S&J's. The S&Js are related to Linearology class. Our stretches and jumps require regulator program modifications. The regulator controls the pitch of the stretch to how high the jump is. It will be hard to control atmospheric pressure if it is above or below what was programmed. I am not particularly good with my calcs. I know I need to work on them, but it is just so boring.

Miss Ram-Y asked us to lower our retraction point to -0.003. I did that. Then she said to jump. I jumped. Nothing happened. I raised my hand and waited for help. I watched every student jump and jump and jump. I lowered my arm and double-checked my chemical titration knob that controls the retraction systoles.

$$-0.003$$

I jumped. Again, nothing happened.

Miss Ram-Y walked by but was talking to another student. I raised my hand to get her attention. Then continued to watch every other student jump and jump and jump.

Miss Ram-Y did not see me. I turned to Poli, my friend who was working next to me, and asked for help, but she just shrugged. She didn't know what I was doing wrong.

I thought about maybe going over to Degmo, but he was all the way across the room. I decided it was better to just go up to Miss Ram-Y herself when she said, "Excellent, everyone. Now let's change that point to +1.302. Everyone went, "WHOA." I couldn't get the first one right, but somehow this next exercise was more exciting.

I went back to my regulator and fidgeted with the chemical titration knob, and countered the retraction with the diastolic indicator, which would change the value to +1.302.

"Everyone, ready? Now lift your right leg and stretch it out behind you. Lean forward with your left arm and crouch down. Yes, Werlo! Yes, Degmo! Yes, Poli!" Miss Ram-Y started walking around again.

This time she was stopping to congratulate students that had made successful transitions.

When she got to me, she stopped. "Fevah, what are you doing?" I was on my right knee with my left arm behind me and my right arm trying to push up and was getting nowhere. I couldn't get back to my regulator to adjust because I couldn't move!

The room vacuumed up all the sound as everyone stopped their wonderful transitions and stared at me. I wanted to hide in a crater and die.

The bell rang, and I was stuck to the floor. Miss Ram-Y told me to wait a few minutes and dismissed the rest of the class. When they finally left, Miss Ram-Y flicked a few switches on my regulator and released me from my position.

"Fevah, what happened?"

I explained what happened, and then... Yes, yes, that happened... I cried. I didn't understand. She told me to come in early tomorrow morning to show the parts I know how to do, and she'll help me with the rest.

If she had only seen me earlier when I was asking for help, I wouldn't be in this mess to begin with. I know it's not her fault, but it's easier to blame her than to admit I suck at this programming.

My bravery evaporated with the rising of the first sun. I could barely concentrate in my classes, and in between them, I avoided any form of social interaction, especially with Degmo. This wasn't that hard to do, considering he was focused on preparing the choreo for his final tryout.

I stayed after school to practice my choreo. I was having a tough time. The tempo was getting away from me, and I was struggling to stay above frequency. There were flaws with almost every move and position. My toe wouldn't complete a loop, and my left leg shook. My arms wouldn't point, and my hips didn't turn. My perfect choreo was falling apart. Not only that, but I also needed frequent breaks when my live-beat adapter sped up, which tripped a few circuits and required a low-level restart.

I'd never make it. Who am I kidding? Those Traditionals didn't know anything. They were just trying to be nice and flatter the youngling.

I sagged down to the ground in frustration. How am I supposed to make it to the L-Hite Dance Squad if I can't dance?

My positions were worse than below Entry Level 2. I wasn't 3750 years old anymore, and I needed to show them I could be 105000 years old and dancing at a Level 2 or 3. The only way to fast-track from Above Quarter 1 to Level 1 is to make it to the L-Hite Dance Squad. Then to make it to GGDC, assuming I can change Miss Ram-Y's mind. My other hand, which wasn't holding up my miserable thoughts, punched my leg.

"Well, hmmm, that looks like a lovely dance," Miss Ram-Y called out to me from the door. I didn't see her come in and jumped.

"Hi, Miss Ram-Y. I was just working out a position change." I lied

94

and stood up.

"Well, you will not figure it out from the floor. The best thing to do is to *do* it," she said.

"That's the problem. I can't *do* it." I blurted out in frustration.

I can't do anything.

"The only way to figure out what you *can't do*, hmmm, is to figure out how far you can take the *can do* parts." She offered and disappeared as quickly as she appeared.

That was the problem, *I can't do anything!* I packed up my things and left.

Yesterday seemed so long ago now. Why was it so easy to dance yesterday?

Was it as electrifying as I thought?

Was it just my imagination, or perhaps a dream?

Clearly, the Traditionals don't get out much to even think my dance was any good. Yet, I couldn't get them out of my mind.

Carest seemed kind. She knew what to say to make people feel better.

When Midi looked right through me. Like she knew exactly what I was thinking and feeling.

Flexis had the skills, though. Flexis was amazing to watch. Tall and cranky, she gave the impression of a rusty bot but she meteor dove her friends out of this world when she danced. I wonder if I asked her to help if she would. Just as quickly as I thought it, I dismissed it — No… they have better things to do.

I guess my subconscious took control, and I found myself on the way to the Siew Home after leaving school.

I travelled around to the rear to the storage area where I met them yesterday. I paused for a nanosecond in front of the mirror and wondered what sort of magic it held. Nah, keep going. My knees wanted to lock and my live-beat O2 conversion frequencies sped up. I could hear the sound in my ears.

"Oh, you are back, youngling?" Carest called out from the back of

96

the room and turned around to shout through another doorway, "Flexis, Flexis, look who's back!"

"Youngling, my goodness, are we glad to see you again! We don't get many visitors. I guess we owe you an apology for moving into your work area. I didn't realize it was being used. We can use the other room if we are in your way." Midi was seated on the opposite wall to Carest and, also shouted through the same doorway for Flexis.

"We have comnis. I don't know why you don't use it." Flexis said as she floated in and glared at both of her friends. "What do you want?" Carest turned towards me and waited.

"Hello," I squeaked out.

Flexis grunted. "Another social call. I have work to do."

"She works here, Flexis. We are in her space." Midi said. She pulled together some supplies and got up to leave. I didn't want her to.

"No, this is where I store some of the equipment for the outdoors. This is your home. I should be leaving." This was a bad idea. I shouldn't be here. I started backing out.

Bad idea

Midi tipped her head to the side and smiled. "But you just got here. Is everything OK?" I sensed her before I saw her. Carest was beside me, checking my connections just like my mom had done. She opened the panel and was looking to run a system diagnostic. If she did that, I'd be here awhile, and I realized this was a bad idea. "I am fine, really I am."

Oh, my ode's song. What have I done?

"You don't seem fine, youngling. Let me check what is misfiring." Carest pushed Scan, and now I *was* planted here for a bit.

"She used to be a DIS Specialist at Medical Bay," Flexis grumbled. She took a seat instead of leaving the room. "Let her do her thing or she'll be thinking about it for the next millennium." DIS stands for Digital Intelligent Software, and Specialists are the programmers for the equipment used to run the diagnostics. Carest fidgeted some more while Flexis stared at me.

It was Midi who swept over and looked me in the eye. "Something is troubling you. Perhaps we can help."

"Check the titration levels on her boot. When those get too high —
dancer's-foot. Yuck," Flexis called. Carest immediately moved
towards my boot and ran a check.

Midi still stood in front of me, her head still tilted, but no smile. She
was waiting for me to respond. "I was hoping... you... you all...
could tell me what I am doing wrong with my choreo?" I whispered.

Where did my voice go?

"What?!" All three responded.

"I'm sorry. I shouldn't be bothering you. You have important work
to do." I said and tried to move backwards, but my suit was still in
run-diagnostic mode.

"I guess what we should have asked is, why? We saw it yesterday,
and it was lovely." Midi said.

"Yes, lovely." Carest stood up, and stood next to Midi, watching me
with wide eyes twitching to the buttons lighting up on my suit. I

looked from Midi and Carest to Flexis, who was still staring at me.

"How much longer on that diag, Carest?" Flexis asked.

Three minutes.

"Which section of your choreo do you think is *wrong*?" Flexis squinted, stressing the last word, and I flinched. The word echoed through me, and my shoulders sagged.

SIGH

"All of it. Well, not all of it, but most of it. I'm not making my pivots or turns. My stand willows. My tilt is off, and it gets worse from there. I was hoping I could learn the Trewn Tip Pirou?"

Flexis screwed up her face. "And how is doing the TTP going to improve a willow?"

Carest murmured, "Be nice, Flexis. She is still learning."

Midi stepped forward. "Let's see it again. Maybe we missed something."

Dear Future Me,

Age: 5250 Years Old

It's my birthday — well, it was my
birthday — It's now the next day, and
everyone is asleep except for me. I
can't sleep. I am having the best day
— well, I *had* the best day.

It started with pancakes. I LOVE
pancakes. Pancakes with syrup, pancakes with chocolate chips,
pancakes with jelly. Pancakes with chocolate sauce.

OMOS! Pancakes!

Oops, that was loud.

Since it's Change Tide 2 and so hot, Degmo's mom took us to a
new shade park. This shade park is a new attraction site, so
there were many people there. I heard my mom and dad
talking about it, and apparently, it's trying to keep Echo Rise
people here instead of having them all go to K-Sed. It's
supposed to be good *tombism* or something like that.

Tourism, not Tombism, sorry!

The park has, like, a millennium of viridian tree groves pods with multi-coloured lights that change with the sound of music.

The music from each pod played interplanetary sounds. There was music, too, from all over the galactic-verse. Fast, slow, legacy, revisional, or contemporary. Lounger seaters were everywhere so people could sit and listen and watch the Doppler wavelengths change with the sound.

Umi Nor and Neptune music sounded loud, like crashing and rubbing stones together. The lights were white, and they flashed a lot. I was expecting to hear roars of thunder, but it wasn't like that at all. My eyes kept closing after every crash, and the flashing lights hurt my eyes.

Degmo, however — LOVED — it.

He jumped and shook his head like many other kids were doing. Because it was my birthday, I told him we had to go, or he could have stayed there for hours.

There was another pod with music from Alpha Strait. It was hard to describe, except to say that it made me feel itchy. Itchy, I know, right? It kind of sounded like the dust from the

blind pikes had been packed together into a ball and then rolled along the floor to crash into a wall. The lights slowly changed between yellow and brown with supersonic blasts of sounds that created black or dark green-like shadows. Degmo's mom found it peaceful, and it was, but like I said, it just made me feel itchy, and the shadows were a little creepy.

Another pod was silver with a grey checked pattern with diamond reflections that sparkled and glittered around us whenever we moved an arm or a foot or even shook our head. The music was slow, with swift melody changes that slowed and moved to another smooth sound, like the sound of juice that I spilled on the counter but louder with low frequencies of clapping glass. I thought it was wonderful, and I wanted to stay there. Degmo put his finger in his mouth like it was the most disgusting thing to experience, but it was my birthday and he had to wait!

The music felt like I was floating. Like it could make the softest bed that I wanted to lie in forever. My legs wanted to move and dance to it. It had a traditional ancient sound, and I didn't know if my type of dancing would have worked. I didn't give it more thought than that because I fell asleep. If it wasn't for Degmo kicking my boot to say let's go.

GRRR

The music was from K-Sed. K-Sed! Who would have thought? I thought all their music was BLAH, but I guess I was wrong.

Degmo's mom took us for the first moon meal, and we had... wait for it...

Pancakes!

Degmo knows how much I love them, and it was his idea — they didn't know I had a whole bucket full already. I ate a plate full of syrup, chocolate sauce, white cream, sprinkles, berries, and honey. I was in pancake paradise.

By then, it was getting dark, and my mom made maladona, an Earth dish from a tropical country like ours. It was red with spices that bit into my tongue and made my eyes water, but it was delish! I licked my fingers and drank a lot of milk. I am feeling hungry again! I think I'll go to the kitchen and see if there are any leftovers.

It's almost my first sun meal. I wonder if my mom will make pancakes. Did I mention I love pancakes?

The Traditionals backed up, and I selected a song from my comni, Celestial Light. Everyone knows that song, and it was easy to match my choreo. I ran through the sequences and stumbled where I expected to and couldn't control any transition sequences. Nothing changed!

"Turn off the music and face the mirror," Flexis said.

I looked at Midi and Carest like it was a joke, but they both nodded. I turned and did what she asked.

"Now dance."

I false-started a few times, but once I found my rhythm, I didn't falter, and I completed all the positions and sequences.

HMMM

I *think* I understood.

"Where would you add the Trewn Tip Pirou?" Midi asked.

Flexis was still giving me the squinted stare. Carest clasped her hands and was beaming.

I responded to Midi but was looking at Flexis. "I think between the Scrall Pull and the Long Point."

Carest stared off for a few moments and nodded. Midi liked it too, but Flexis shook her head.

"Or… or, I could add it at the end, as a grand finale sequence," I suggested.

Flexis shook her head. She did not agree with that proposal either.

 106

"You start with it. That'll get their attention. Stand back and watch," said Flexis.

"Flexis, this isn't good for your joints." Carest wrung her hands.

Flexis ignored her friend, and for the next few minutes stole my breath. Flexis performed my choreo and included the Trewn Tip Pirou as she recommended - at the beginning. She paused after the step as a small smile appeared on her face. When she was done, I clapped without waiting a beat longer.

"That was amazing! How did you do it?" I asked.

Flexis replied, "I didn't. *You* did. Well, I added a touch of my seasoning, and that is it. It is yours. That is how it looks." Flexis was moonbeam tall, and I didn't realize how tall she was until she bent down and repeated that last sentence inches from my face.

"Bu-but my choreo doesn't look like that."

"Yes, it does. It looks exactly like it. We just have some tidying to do. Every masterpiece, whether it is a dance performance or a majestic structure, requires adjustments. I know what the issue is with your dance performance," said Flexis, and she held up her finger.

Midi and Carest looked at her with surprise.

"The song. The song you chose is all wrong."

"But everyone knows that song. It's quite popular for dance choreos in competitions." I replied.

"Just because it's common doesn't mean it suits you. You are not common, are you?" Carest responded with a wink.

UMMM

Yes, no, yes. I have no idea anymore…

Carest wondered what song I should use instead, and the three Traditionals debated and flung song names at me and ignored my response. There was a Great Lament for Umi Nor Planet, Majestic Trilogy, by a brilliant musician on Alpha Strait. They debated using a great musical primary from Earth – Drake. But the nanosecond Carest suggested it, they all shook their heads.

Then the song from my dream poked at me. "What about Raglan Chrome?" I asked. I didn't even realize I knew the name. They weren't listening, and I repeated it louder. Still no response.

"WHAT ABOUT RAGLAN CHROME?" I asked for the third time, and they turned with wide eyes.

"Yes!"

"Although you didn't need to shout about it," said Flexis.

"Yes, youngling, that is perfect," said Carest.

Midi checked her comni and found the song. "But first," she said and spun across the room, letting her long cape wrap her up. Between twirls, she continued her thought. "Listen to the song. Listen to the curves and arcs and the wisdom." She was beautiful to watch. "It's full of hope and surprise. Dreams and plans. Love and magic."

The Traditionals moved into their own interpretations of the dance. I watched, fascinated, as they leapt, twirled, swept, and flowed. It was one of the prettiest things I have ever seen, and I hoped it wasn't a dream. Even if it were, this was one I wouldn't mind staying in longer.

When the song ended, they bowed low and burst into applause for each other.

Flexis stopped and turned to me. "Start with the Trewn Tip Pirou." I waited for the music to start and waited some more. I was about to turn it on from my comni, but Flexis interrupted, "Do it *without* the music first. Let them see the fast footfall, then follow it up with the melody of Raglan."

I fumbled several times and Flexis adjust my posture and gravitational offset. "You'll need a bit more practice on that, but keep going," Flexis muttered.

Midi and Carest disappeared into the back of the quardome. I couldn't see them, but I knew they were there watching. When Midi spoke up, it startled us. "Start with doing it in front of the mirror first."

I did as she asked. The positions and transition flowed easily, and it

felt wonderful. At the end, Carest stood up and clapped. "Perfect score!"

Midi added, "Now turn around and face us, but don't see us. See yourself in the mirror like you did just now. That is what we are. We are the mirror of your performance. If you scowl, we'll scowl. If you smile, we smile. If you are confident, we have confidence in you. What you fling out always comes back to you."

From the moment my toe scraped the ground for the Trewn Tip Pirou, a spark ignited. My image reflected in the mirror like stars.

The Trewn Tip Pirou is like lighting a match. It starts with a quick brush, followed by several swift footfalls, like the dancing fire from a spark.

BOOM!

It's typically a transitory movement, and to start the dance with a transitory movement is unheard of. Therefore, Flexis thought it was more exciting that way, going from an unexpected move to the expected.

My legs felt strong and bold and drew a roadmap to the root of my soul. The ribbons of melody in Raglan Chrome pushed my desire like the speed of light through a quantum leap. My arms circled and drew in my every dream, and then pushed and spun them out into the chasm of the galactic-verse.

As the tune sped towards the bridge, I repeated the Trewn Tip Pirou, but faster—staccato triple time. Then the jump and double spin of the Scrall Pull and ended with the full leg extension of the Long Point.

I stared at my reflection until I caught my breath. Every part of me was brimming with energy. Any fear I had evaporated in that moment, and all I saw was a bright path toward my dreams.

Dear Future Me,

Age: 1500 Years Old

Mr Kex, my language teacher, says I am exceptionally good at picking up different galactic dialects. He said it's important when we travel to communicate with different lifeforms, so we don't get tricked. He said that when we are tourists in

a foreign landmass, we should speak to other lifeforms in their language. They feel happy and want to help us if we get lost.

He also said that there are over one million languages and dialects spoken across the galactic-verse, and very few lifeforms can speak to them all. The only exception is computer bots. They know every language, including their own binary code.

When I grow up, I want to be the only one in all the galactic-verse to speak ALL these languages. I want to travel to all the planets and kingdoms.

I plan to do a lot of travelling.

Kings and Queens of kingdoms will invite me to dance for them. I will win every trophy and be a one hundred times Great-Galactic Dance Competition winner.

I will be supernova famous.

That's what my mom said. She said she saw it in a dream. But I knew that already. She said that I need to record a message every year until my 7500th birthday, so that I know what I am supposed to do and not forget. So that is what I am doing. I don't think I will forget that I am going to be famous, rich, talented, and so pretty, like a queen in her diamond kingdom.

Every planet will want me to dance for them. They will send me zillions of credits and buckets of gold, and I will tell them, "No, no, no, I only dance for Echo Rise." Echo rise will name vectors after me. Ram-Y Dance Academy will name a practice hall... NOOO... a dance sector after me.

Oh, my ode's song, even better, I will make my own school and call it Fevah's Dance Academy, and I will teach the classes. I will be just like Miss Ram-Y. Miss Ram-Y and I will be best friends, and she will come to learn more things.

YES!

I will win all the trophies and the GGDC and then build a school just for the best kids like me. I will teach dance all day and not make anyone learn about ancient topographies or intergalactic battles. I will get Mr. Kex to teach language at my school, and he'll tell everyone how I was his best student.

Degmo could be my helper teacher. He is good at helping students do stuff, and he's really nice to the ones that get sad, like me sometimes. He'd be the best at it. He also knows a lot of stuff because his parents are Sentinels, and they know a lot of stuff that is going on in our galactic verse. He would be perfect for the job, and he's my best friend!

I will travel to the other galaxies on my private transport ship.

SWOOSH

And wake up only after the second sun.

Wait!

If I am in charge of the school, then I'd teach and be there when the kids get there. So, I have to get up before the first sun. No way! I will change that.

School only starts after the second sun. Everyone sleeps in.

The Great-Galactic Dance Competition is starting in a few days, and I am supernova excited. I want to see all the best dancers show off their skills. I know how to do all their dances, so when I am older, it will be so easy. I don't know why you have to be 7500 years old just to try out for the L-Hite Dance Squad. Their choreos are so easy, I can do it now. But I must wait.

I bet if I tried out now, I'd make the squad, and then I could tell Miss Ram-Y we are going to the GGDC. She would say yes because I am the best student.

Mr. Kex just told me I was the best one. Well, in Language - but it's the same thing.

The next day, I reserved a rehearsal dance quarzone and practiced until my nerves stopped being nervous. It was only during my last break, and once I turned off the music, and all the *Hope and Surprise. Dreams and Plans. Love and Magic* that Midi said Raglan Chrome expressed had dissolved, leaving me feeling lonely. I hadn't talked to Degmo in days.

The last few days were an electromagnetic radiation of emotions with fluctuating electric and magnetic fields that caused feelings to grow quickly like blind pikes during Change Tide 1. I bet Degmo wouldn't admit it, but I know he was going through it, too.

I missed Degmo's company. Ever since we were 1500 years old, we've been best friends. We talked every day at school and always after we did our homework. We were both going through some hard stuff, and I hope he missed my company as much as I missed his. I decided to one-link him so we could meet up and talk at TCP – The Commons Practice Hall.

My rehearsal dance quarzone space was small and had become extremely hot. If I stayed any longer, I would be well within the zone of short-circuiting something important. When I moved to the larger TCP, I shook off my shell suit and left it in a heap on the floor.

My body followed it shortly after as I slumped to the floor to cool down. I stared up at the rounded ceiling, wondering why on Echo Rise was this room designed like this. That is how Degmo found me. He brought over a bag of brittle faiza, my favourite! Small salty globs of sweet, yummy goodness!

Degmo said he was scouring old footage of GGDCs to find a few new routine sets. I gulped, and a faiza felt lodged in my throat.

118

Degmo lay down next to me and sighed. "If I don't make it… I don't know what I'll do." He paused, and I thought he was looking at the ceiling wondering why it was designed that way too, when he continued. "That's all I can think about. I don't even think I am sleeping. I can't wait until it is over…. You know what I mean?" I nodded and agreed with him.

It's quite out of character for me, but after yesterday's session with the Traditionals, I was enjoying a strange calm that was opposite to my natural state of general panic and impatience. I guess he noticed and looked sideways at me suspiciously. "Why are *you* not freaking out?"

I shrugged. Besides practicing until I melted, I guess I was as ready as I was going to be, and this left me feeling amazingly comfortable and not freaked out at all. It sort of felt like I was drifting through the galactic-verse, hovering, watching myself through each move and yet, experiencing it at the same time. I didn't tell him that, though; it sounded weird.

Degmo and I have always shared each other's secrets and dreams, hopes, and fears and it didn't feel right not to tell him about my

Traditional friends. I opened my mouth, hoping a sound or a word would inspire the rest of the story, but nothing came out. To be honest, the story almost didn't sound real.

Maybe the Traditionals aren't real and they are a figment of my stressed-out imagination. Could I be that anxious?

Degmo sensed my hesitation and decided he was going to continue with the inquisition. He propped himself up on his elbow and looked over at me. "Fevah, I know there is something you are not telling me."

"I guess I am getting nervous and don't want to talk about it. Hey, you did the same thing to me," I deflected.

He wrinkled his nose and sniffed the air, "I smell a gaseous expulsion of…"

I laughed aloud. "Okay, okay, I've been practicing super hard and trying something new. I'm too nervous to think about it."

"New?"

"I changed the song. It's fine. I like it better." I said, trying to make it sound like it was no big deal. I wanted to show him, but it also seemed like I would reveal a tremendous secret if I did.

His first performance was amazing. I can only imagine what his next one would be. I wondered if I was going to be as good, or dare I hope, better? I was losing some of my bravery as I let the chill of doubt in again – I thought I closed that door! I should have kept to myself and continued to practice.

"Fine, don't tell me. I probably don't want to know," Degmo rolled his eyes and moved back to the wall, stretching his legs. I felt guilty. I opened my mouth to make words of confession again, but nothing happened.

So, instead, I asked him how his second dance choreo was coming along. I was curious about what I would compete with. "Do you want to see it?" he asked.

I nodded, and he told me to play Tessie's Solar Moon.

Phew

It wasn't Raglan Chrome, but a much more modern synth drop. I queued the song, and off he spun.

It was even *better* than the last one. He looked confident and strong, and I wondered if he felt the same way I did yesterday when I danced to Raglan Chrome - like he was the centre of the galactic-verse too.

Oh, my ode's song. I am doomed.

Degmo bowed, and I clapped. I congratulated and assured him he'd make the team. I could see he was on the verge of asking to see my dance, which, of course, I didn't want to show him right now. I looked at my comni and excused myself, saying my parents were looking for me.

That night I didn't sleep. Instead, I practiced my choreo until the rise of the first sun. At first, I walked through the position of the movements and then counted in my head. Then, since I was already awake, I got up and tip-toed through the choreo, making sure not to bump or knock anything over. My parents would be pretty upset if they knew I was still up.

When the sky changed colours, my live-beat adapter took off like a goop as I took several large breaths and got ready for the big day.

My mom wished me good luck as I headed out the door, and I knew - I felt - her eyes boring deep into my soul but I wouldn't turn around. This meant too much to me right now. This wasn't the time to get emotional.

SNIFF - SNIFF

I will not cry.

I stood in the forum with the students from shortlist and was nervous as Nelly the Autobotter, our class-pet, who peed every time someone looked at her.

Miss Ram-Y came in, tapping her toe to a beat only she could have understood, and we shuffled around nervously. "You've all been given numbers. I will pick one out of the box to start." She reached in and pulled out a small piece of paper. "1417?" Miss Ram-Y announced. That was my number.

The room went still.

"What will you be performing for us today, Fevah?"

My eyes widened as I saw my competitors staring back at me.

Body and mind respond to Dos not to Thinks...

The only way to figure out what you can't do...

Just because it's common doesn't mean it suits you. You are not common, are you?...

We are the mirror to your performance. If you scowl, we'll scowl. If you smile, we smile. If you are confident, we have confidence in you. What you fling out always comes back to you. ...

Miss Ram-Y looked up from her board, impatient for me to start. "Fevah, quickly please!" Behind her I could see Degmo giving me a small wave and a smile of support.

See the mirror.

"Please play Raglan Chrome," I said, nodding to the music director, "But wait for my cue before starting it." There were mutters and whispers, repeating the title and my instructions along the benches.

Raglan Chrome is a beautiful and slow song. It was the song that fanned the embers in my dream. It was the song the Traditionals said I should use.

I turned the knob to slow my live-beat adapter. This would hopefully stabilize and regulate by OPE rates in case my calculations were above margin outputs.

My toe licked the ground to start the first sequence of the Trewn Tip Pirou. Then I nodded to the music director and felt the rush of melody fill the room to Raglan Chrome.

Minutes fell aside like seconds as I executed each position, transition, overlay, extension, and spin with accuracy and precision. I did not wobble, willow, or misstep.

When the music ended, I dropped to the floor into a leg extension Long Point and waited for several seconds. I was expecting to hear a shuffle to stand up and applause. Instead, I heard the soft whirring of an overcharged respirator.

No one clapped.

No one whooped.

Nobody did anything for a while.

The music director jumped to action in the silence and started a clap, hoping to encourage the others, but it fell flat when he looked over to Miss Ram-Y.

Miss Ram-Y was looking down. Did she even look up? Did she see anything at all? All eyes were on Miss Ram-Y. There would be no reaction until she commented.

"Raglan Chrome. That is an interesting selection, hmmm. Why did you choose it?" she asked.

"I like the melody," I replied.

Miss Ram-Y nodded. That was all.

I walked off the stage, and the tears that I had been holding back since before first sun, finally burst out.

SOB

It was terrible.

I was terrible.

I shouldn't have listened to those Traditionals!

Maybe I *am* still sick. Maybe I am delirious with a celestial illness, and this is all in my imagination. If so, then it's time to wake up.

WAKE UP

I should have stayed home. I knew I was going to mess this up.

I always do.

Miss Ram-Y called another number, and I decided I wasn't going back to watch. I wasn't anyone's competition. I ran home.

I was miserable. I wasn't *just* miserable — I was humiliated. I wanted to move to another galaxy!

I'm going to quit.

I came home, shut my door, and it stayed that way for the rest of the night while I willed my body to be transported to another dimension.

My sister buzzed in to use my computer pod, and I threw the biggest book I could find at the door.

THUNK

The sound shook the wall, which made me feel better for the moment.

My mom linked into my audio stream and asked me what had happened. I told her about the disaster, then disconnected before she could say anything. I knew what she would say, and I really didn't want to hear it.

This was her fault.

She shouldn't have let me do this. She should have stopped me at the door this morning. She shouldn't have filled my head with crazy dreams that cursed me into thinking I was something better than I will ever be.

I am a miserable failure.

My comni blipped with incoming alerts on the one-link channel with

Degmo. I didn't care what he had to say. I didn't want to hear about how great his last dance was or about anyone else's, for that matter.

Ok, full disclosure, I was a little curious, but if I talked to him, I would have to hear about how well *he* did.

I am a terrible friend. I turned off my communicator and went to bed.

The next day I couldn't avoid him. He slid up to me during our first break, "I think Werlo Cus will make it." Degmo pointed his chin toward Werlo. "She's good. Maybe even Nea, Werlo's friend, but I don't know, I didn't think she did that great." He leaned over to give me a little nudge. "Sorry you're bummed, Fevah. I thought it was awesome."

"Yeah," I responded with my voice just above a whisper. If I said any more, I knew my tears would find their way out again. We continued eating our snack in silence.

The next two days were more of the same. I did eventually ask Degmo how he did, and he thought he did OK. "But there was a lot of competition. I don't know why you think you did badly. Well, I guess I know why you *think* you did, but it's not true. You did awesome. You may have blown us all away. Where did you learn how to do those transitions, anyway?" I shrugged and said I did some research.

The rest of our conversations were small gossip bits from Degmo about what he heard around school, followed by one-word responses from me.

I avoided the Siew Home and called in sick again when I was supposed to work. I didn't care if they fired me.

I didn't care much about much.

But I think what truly kept me away was that I didn't know how to tell Midi, Carest, and Flexis that I had failed. They would be so disappointed in me.

Dear Future Me,

Age: 3000 Years Old

I know I should have recorded this last week, but I was too mad. I think I still am a bit, but I'm all grown up now, so I guess I understand. Let me tell you about it, and you can decide now that you — well, me ... I — I am older now.

I am the best dancer at home and at school. Everyone says I am. My teachers, my friends, everyone. I don't do it because everyone says I am but because I really, really like it.

No! I love it.

It's the best feeling on the entire planet. I love it so much that I will be the next youngling, well, competitor?... competitAtor? ... Competitor sounds better. The next competitor to be sent to the Great-Galactic Dance Competition. It's been a hundred millennia since Echo Rise was represented, and I will be the next one to do it. I know it. I feel it.

My mom thinks she even had a dream about it, but my mom is so old now, almost a Traditional, so I am not sure if she remembers it. I am not even sure she remembers I dance. I am not sure if she remembers I am the best dancer anyone has ever seen.

Ok, so I am getting ahead of myself. I guess I am still pretty mad.

My sister Luleh is 2250 years younger than me. I am the older sister, and I am supposed to give everything to her.

Share!

Share everything with her. I don't get to keep anything for myself. Everything is 'ours.' Nothing is 'mine.' Not even my dreams.

Luleh likes to read. She doesn't dance. She hates dancing. She is barely passing her subjects in her level placements, and no one seems to care. My parents just keep saying that she'll figure it out soon, and all I remember is them both telling me to try harder when I came home with a poor grade.

However, Luleh has been researching an Earther craft called puppeteering. She is wrapping old socks and shells around her hands, drawing scary faces, and then talking to them, or they

132

talk to each other. It's creepy and I think we should run a chemical diagnostic on her, but everyone — including my parents — thinks it's cute.

During the Change Tide 2 break, my dad was looking for a project to do around our quarzone. My mom whispered something to him, and off he went to build it. I had offered to help, but they both shook their heads.

They wanted it to be a surprise.

With my birthday coming up, I was excited. After a few weeks, the design became obvious. It was a stage. A long, flat white stage with 50 white light bulbs all around it. I saw him evaluating it out, and I felt like I was lit from the inside out when he turned them on.

I couldn't wait to test it out.

On my birthday, they covered my eyes and walked me over to it. When they uncovered them, my heart sang. It was wonderful. I ran onto the stage and twirled, jumped, and rolled across every square inch. It was my first stage.

This is a sign.

My next stage will be even bigger, but it all starts with this one. I stayed on it all day until after the first moon meal. After I finished my meal, I heard voices coming from my stage. My sister was on it, with her freaky-looking puppets.

I told her to get off, and she ignored me.

I went up to her and told her to get off, and she ignored me again.

I pulled her creepy rag dolls off her hands and threw them off the stage. She couldn't ignore me anymore. Instead, she screamed and cried — the baby.

My parents were not happy with me and told me I had to share it. There's that word again. Share. I had to share it because it was for both of us.

WHAT?!

I was in complete shock. I thought it was my birthday present. I got off the stage and didn't get back on it for a few days, which suited Luleh just fine because she could now have it all to herself.

It was so not fair.

Yesterday, my dad came over to talk to me about it. He said he was pretty sad that I wasn't using the stage that he had built for me.

For me? I thought you said I had to share it.

He nodded and understood how I felt. He said a bunch of boring grown up words that didn't help me feel any better. I told him I'd think about it.

He said something that was not interesting, but the more I thought about it, the more it made sense, but I wouldn't admit that to him. He said, "When the suns rise, they show us where we are going. When they set, they show us how far we've come. Someday you'll understand that, Fevah."

GRRR

The Someday word again.

This time, the someday was yesterday when I realized I knew where I was going, but that Luleh needed a bit of help to figure

135

that out.

Now, that doesn't mean that I am happy to share my birthday present with her, but I love my sister, and I want her to find something that makes her as happy as dancing makes me. If that's creepy puppets, then it's creepy puppets, but I really hope it isn't.

The next morning, I checked my messages.

Degmo, Degmo, Degmo, Carest, Degmo…

Wait, what? Carest?

I pressed play and watched the message. "Youngling, Flexis, Midi and I are beside ourselves. How did your tryout go? *Shhh, Flexis, I am asking her…* Flexis is wondering how you executed Trewn Tip Pirou? Please come by and let us know." The pit in my stomach grew bigger.

How do I tell them I was a galactic failure?

I didn't want to work today — I was too jittery. I also didn't want to see Midi, Carest, or Flexis. It would be easier if I showed up tomorrow, after the results, to tell them I didn't make it. That would be easier than explaining how badly the tryout went yesterday.

But I had missed several days already, and guilt was setting in. I also didn't want to be a 'Blate' who was summoned to their quardomes just to be dismissed and leave my job in shame. I couldn't handle that right now. So, I thought if I showed up earlier than they expected, I could go unnoticed. Right after school, I gravicombusted over - I wish I had a goop!

Once at the Siew Home, I crept in and didn't dare look around. I heard humming, and my eyes refused to follow the sound, but my curiosity let me down. Midi was at a desk, working on a large project. By large, it wasn't so much the effort, but the size. The project took up the full room. She took several steps back to study shelf placement and went back to the desk to write something down. All the while, she hummed to herself.

Traditionals sit on their benches, dip their brushes in vessels and build. It can take many moons to build a structure. The older the

Traditional, the more complicated the design.

I gulped down my anxiety. I should wait until tomorrow, but what if she saw me outside? I should tell her now and get ahead of the inevitable inquisition. She'll tell Carest and Flexis, and no one would be surprised by the results. I didn't dare let myself think about the disappointment.

Midi's head was down, entering some data. When she looked up, she picked a brush and drew a bar, then another across that one. Her head moved back and forth between her desk and the structure.

I approached her with my neck stretching, trying to glimpse what she was working on. "Hi," I said.

She turned to me and smiled, "Hi there, youngling."

I smiled back and looked down at the ground. I didn't know how to start this conversation, but she did. "Well, now. Have you ever seen a Nerg Zone constructed?"

I shook my head.

139

"It seems easy enough. Three angles, three sides. It should all fit together. She pointed to two spots on the panel and said she wanted the light to come through here. "But the angle has to be just right, so the light is not direct, or it will burn the greenie shell inside."

"The panels will stretch if I shrink this side. I've torn this down and rebuilt it at least," she held up her fingers and counted, "three-times."

She continued to talk while she tilted and measured panel after panel. "The first time was a trial. I wanted to see how it looked. I put a flower in it, and it burnt. I checked my data analyzers, and the angle was correct; everything seemed correct. Strange. So, I tried again, and this time I changed the angle. It burnt. Same outcome. Very bizarre. I decided it was the thickness, not the angle. It still burnt. Goodness! Well now, what could it be?

I showed it to a friend, and he said that the angle was incorrect. Can't be, I huffed. I checked my values. Can't be. We debated it for a while. I love a good fight. But then we decided it was the *type* of flower I used. I selected a different species, and it worked!

The problem is, now I need to create another one that will help the

first greenie species grow. I am not sure how to solve it, but I have enough experience to figure it out. The hard part is trusting myself and thinking it through." Was Midi speaking to the secret in my heart or to the actual situation?

Midi put down her pen and glasses and asked, "Now that you've listened to my problems, do you want to tell me yours?"

I told her about the tryout and Miss Ram-Y's reaction. When I was done, she blinked at me a few times and prodded, "And?"

"And what? That's the end."

She blinked a few times. "The end? The end of what?"

I recognize she is a Traditional, but is she losing her galactic marbles, "The end of the story."

"The end of the story? That is not possible. You haven't received the results. There is no end to that story."

"I know how it ends," I muttered.

"Youngling, there are a lot of things to feel sad about, but imagining a tragic ending is just that... imagination. Imagination is something to fill the gap between two truths."

She didn't understand.

"When will you learn the results?" Midi asked.

"I think tomorrow," I said.

"Well, alright. Let's wait before we foretell any doom. Promise me that. If Flexis sees you like this...." Midi rolled her eyes and gave my hand a tight squeeze. "Wait for the ending. Don't predict the end because you imagine it."

Before my mouth knew I was even thinking about it, the question that had been burning my curiosity tumbled out. "Midi, did you know Aubry Trewn?"

"Of course, I did. She was older than me. She was wonderful to watch. Have you seen any of her performances?" Midi asked.

"It's been hard to find. The Sentinel database says she was the last competitor we sent to the GGDC, but it says nothing about where

142

she is now. Do you know?"

Midi tilted her head and thought about it for a few nanoseconds. "You know, I am not sure. But I am sure Flexis knows. She was her understudy."

"Really?!"

Midi gave me her lopsided smile and suggested I ask Flexis about it sometime.

"Regardless of what Miss Ram-Y says, Fevah, I saw you dance, and you are a very capable dancer. Carest, Flexis and me, we can all see your potential. It's time that you see it, too."

I nodded, but I didn't really understand. How could they think I had any talent?

Midi sensed my confusion and typed a few words into her comni and projected the results. "Have you ever heard of a Boomerang?"

I shook my head, but the word sounded familiar. I looked at the projection of the funny-shaped tool. Midi explained, "A boomerang is a prehistoric tool found in the Milky Way Galaxy on Planet Earth." I nodded because everyone knew where Earth was located.

Midi continued, "The boomerang was used as a hunting tool by nomadic tribes. It was a small, strange-looking tool, but it was mighty. It could take down very large, dangerous beasts. Only people with great skill could master this tool." Midi changed the image to a video of how it worked, from the spinning throw going way off into the distance and returning to the hand that threw it.

"The skill is tricky. Throw it exactly right, or it will not come back to you. If you throw it badly, it could miss its target, or worse, hurt someone or even you."

She showed me a few more videos of it missing its target and getting lost in trees and grasses and other ones of its injuries. "In this video, this earthling wasn't ready... wasn't prepared to catch the returned arc, and it hurt him... badly."

Ouch!

She turned off the projection and looked at me. "Your intentions are

like that boomerang. If you are unsure or afraid of it, it will not go far or not come back. More importantly, when you throw it out there, you need to be ready to catch it when it returns to you. If not, then you shouldn't have thrown it."

Dear Future Me,

Age: 7500 Years Old

When I was 1500 years old, I was
run over by a toy commuter nub.
Degmo and I were having a great
time swinging, sliding, and
throwing discs into the quadgrove.

Our circuits were overheating, so we
took my toy goop to the confectionery to buy an Icy - Nebula's
Ripple.

Oh, my ode's song, my favourite!

On our way back to the quadgrove, some kids were playing with
their toy nub. We moved to the side to let them pass, but they
kept bouncing and talking. The next thing we realized, they
drove into and over me, knocking the treat out of my hand
and leaving tire marks across my suit.

They laughed and kept going. When I stood up, I picked up a
rock to throw at them, but I hesitated. They got away when I
stopped to think about where to aim. I wasn't hurt, but I was
angry.

147

I often wonder what could have happened if I had thrown that rock. I have several go-to scenarios. In one, I would hit the girl driving and she would fall out of her nub the same way she knocked me off my goop, and I would bounce over her a few times. Other times, I throw the rock, and the nub breaks in half. A few times, I imagine their heads ejecting from their bodies, but that is usually saved for my more creative moments.

I don't know why I was thinking about that this morning. I guess it was the way that day made me feel. I was having an enjoyable day, a fun day, a fun time, when something stole it from me. I could have been hurt, but I wasn't. I was just so... so... furious! I wanted to hurt and destroy. I didn't throw the rock and I remember hesitating, but that is not true.

I am embarrassed to think about what I could have done in my anger.

What really happened is that Degmo grabbed my arm and pulled it down. I remember yelling at him, screaming at him, I was so angry that he stopped me from hurting them.

He just grinned and waited for me to calm down. When all I could see was the small puff cloud from their get-away nub craft, he finally said, "Fevah, you're fine and I'm fine. I didn't

want to spend the rest of the day fighting with them. Let's get another Ripple, my treat!

Degmo was right. I never told him that, though. I wanted the icy.

He was right to ignore those kids. I wasn't hurt, and we were having so much fun. We got two more icy and spent the rest of the day bouncing and climbing rooted tall greenies.

In three months, we will try out for the L-Hite Dance Squad. One or both of us will make it. It's been my dream for so long, and as the days and years have moved along that dream, I don't feel like I am ready.

I know Degmo is ready. I watch him dance, and it's like the air gets vacuumed out of me. I don't know how to compete with that. I really don't want to compete with that. I don't know how I'd feel if he made the squad—and I didn't. I can't even imagine making the squad myself and not having him there, too.

After a lot of thought, I have concluded that if Degmo makes it and I do not, the plan does not change. I will throw all my energy and time into pressuring Miss Ram-Y to send him to the GGDC. He prevented me from throwing a rock and messing up a perfectly good day.

This time, I'll get him to throw his dream into the galactic-verse and bring home the trophy. His name will fill the blank space on Miss Ram-Y's trophy wall.

Yup, I can do that. I can make that happen. I will be ok with that. I know I will be.

On my way back to my quarzone, after talking with Midi, the memory of the day at the quadgrove slid up to me and I wondered what really would have happened if I had thrown the rock that day. A boomerang would have been helpful, but I would have thrown it in anger, and it would have likely lopped off my head.

If the boomerang was an action, then my performance during the tryout was perfect. It wasn't a flop. The misery I was carrying around with me since that day didn't matter. I know, without a doubt, my feelings were clear and purposeful, and I had done the best I could do. I guess without really thinking about it, a boomerang is what I had thrown into the galactic-verse. My wish, my intent and it looked beautiful spinning out there. What will happen when it comes back to me? Will it come back to me?

Dare I hope?

"Good luck, Fevah."

"Good luck, Deg."

We hugged each other before walking into the rehearsal hall. The silence in the hall seemed heavy. We sat close to each other to provide support while we each quietly hoped for our own successes.

Our comnis buzzed, and we looked up at the giant receptor vision.

It was Miss Ram-Y. "The last few weeks have been very illuminating for several of our dancers, hmmm. They practiced tirelessly to create performances that were both captivating and intriguing." We looked at each other anxiously.

"Selection for the L-Hite Dance Squad has been difficult for me this year, as the talent was overwhelming, hmmm. Before I continue, I would like to show you highlights of some performances."

As images sprang to the screen, I squeezed my eyes tight. I overheard several gasps and giggles, but my eyes remained closed. When I heard Raglan Chrome, I think I must have stopped breathing because my live-beat adapter beeped its warning. The image moved on to another dancer as I lifted my eyelid. It felt like I was encrusted in ice, and if I moved, I would crack.

Keep going. I sighed in my head.

"Isn't this amazing, hmmm?" Miss Ram-Y continued. "Applause, applause, applause! Students, please stand up and take a bow." We shuffled to our feet and bent low, brushing the floor with our fingertips before we stood back up. This was the formal bow reserved only for the stage.

"Now, with pleasure, let's welcome the following talent into the L-Hite Dance Squad: Werlo Cus, Catio Recmo, Degmo Sokz, and Orat Gemen."

I counted the names as she announced them. Four. Students were hugging each other. Degmo turned towards me, waiting for me to be the first to congratulate him, but my fingers were in the air, and I couldn't put them down. She said five would make the Squad, but Miss Ram-Y only said four names.

What's going on?

"Before the celebrations begin, there is another talent that will join the squad. At first, this student confused me." My four fingers were still in the air as I listened. "This student did something so unique that it addled me and that doesn't happen too often." The last sentence garnered whispered giggles along the bench. Miss Ram-Y continued, "But it was necessary to rattle the gates of my memory, hmmm." She laughed at her joke as I am sure many of the Traditionals and Council did.

"Our mastery," she continued, "of Dance, is respected and rewarded across the Galactic-verse. I sometimes underestimate our historical dominance, and the impact it has on our younglings. It reminded me of the meaning at the core of our dance culture.

Magic.

I had forgotten through the millennia our core mantra - faster than the speed of light and lighter than the gamma rays of our suns. This student reminded me it has been a long time since we told the galactic-verse who we are.

Therefore, I am honoured to announce that Fevah Seren will represent Echo Rise at the Great-Galactic Dance Competition this year. Fevah, stand up." I rose with uncertainty and was still holding four fingers in the air. My eyes were wide, I looked to my left and my friends were bowing. I looked to my right and my friends were bowing and through the walls of the rehearsal halls, I heard applause. My feet melted onto the ground like liquid mercury and somewhere from deep inside, I caught the boomerang.

Oh, my ode's song, I am going to Earth!

Fevah's Language Key

Fevah's galaxy is not the same ours and she uses words and phrases that are unfamiliar. Here's a cheat sheet to help you with some words or phrases.

Note: This book is based on imagination. Many words or phrases are not scientifically based, although they may sound like it.

buzzing like a zyme	buzzing like a mosquito
celestial waterfall	chain of unfortunate events
change tides	seasons (change tide 1: cool season; change tide 2: hot season)
chemical regulator	biological element exchange
dance sector	a dance room for practice
dark matter	something difficult
electromagnetic radiation of emotions	lots of emotional things happening at the same time
goop	transportation that leaps to move and is used similar to car
greenie pods	forests
legacy competitors	mature/older dancers
lifeforms	inhabitants of galaxies that range from people to insects
mean crater	a real meanie
meteor dove	crazy, wonderful, out of this world
multi-level capital pods	office buildings

157

nerg zone	triangular greenhouse
neptune hurl	cool/ be cool
nub craft	bus
one-link channel	direct access, no dialling
OPE rates	oxygen polynomial exchange rates. a calculation that converts elements into breathable air.
quadgrove	a playground or park to play
quantum gaming	playing games with kids through the galaxy
quardome	large mansion
quarzone	A home or a room in a home
rosettas & heel pants	cloud shapes
sentinels	news journalists
solar burst in my side	pain in the butt
vangard	new competitors
vector	town/small city

SIGHT

Book 2 in The Great -Galactic Dance
Competition Book Series

The Birch hummed with activity. We walked through the main entrance, called Main Base, and every strand of my hair stood and shook with excitement. It was like walking into a Vector Metros. The chaos cyclones up and hits you like a sharp wind. Carts and drones, cubes, and shells whiz by, being pushed or pulled or colliding into each other. Little armies of passengers and crew are absorbed into this cyclone and follow the activity, laughing, arguing, or are simply overwhelmed by it all.

The chaos is further intensified by an assortment of voices rotated through the speakers, welcoming and providing instructions for help in many languages. One voice says to proceed to an attendant to check in. Another voice was giving the timetable for mealtimes. Yet another voice was advising about weather patterns on Echo Rise in the Gad Nor Sequences, where I am from, followed by the conditions on other planets and galaxies at our next few stops, including our destination of Earth.

My eyes and ears move left and right, up and down, diagonally and in circles, as they absorb this wonderful mayhem. I felt huge and powerful that this will be my domain, but then just as quickly, the world domination ended when the floor we stood on had a life of its own. It faded from a brown and dark grey panel to a blue and white wave that caused me to jump into my mom, who jumped and yanked me back when I slammed into her. A few other new passengers did the same thing until we realized it was just an effect as bright red and green arrows directed passengers to various levels and sections.

Above our heads were 5 levels. Each level held hundreds of Quarzones. There were living quarters, games arcades, cinematic experience platforms, system diagnostics, mineral deconstructions, metallurgic adjudications, travel simulations and on and on.

It was humongous. Even that was an understatement. It was a galaxy within a galaxy and it looked like it was going to be an adventure.

Earlier, when we boarded, we decompressed and equalized our breathing apparatuses as we were led through a long brown and grey hallway. This hallway had really awful yellow blinking lights that kind of made me want to throw up. The lights sanitized our shell suits and whatever cubes and supplies that came with us. We met a Marthian on a trip from Solly Fect, a few million light-years from Echo Rise, who informed us that the 'Sani-Lights' also allowed our vision sensors to sync with the ship's visual arrays. This meant that we had complete control over what we wanted to see and how we saw things on the ship. If it were too bright, we could change our sensors to anti-glare with blue hues, or if it was too dark, we could add a dim light to where we were going. Oh, my ode's song, this was going to be awesome!

The Marthian also told us that The Birch was the largest of the Earthling fleet. There were three other ships, The Oak, The Elm, and the Maple, all named after an Earth horticultural filtration system. Because The Birch was the largest, it was also the slowest and travelled in lower orbital fields. They could do a few quantum jumps, but it still had taken them a few months. The Captain of The Birch hoped traffic was slower this time of year and we could take a few more jumps and spend less time in the lower fields.

My mom and the Marthian continued to chat about the changing weather patterning and Sentinel gossip, and I lost interest and checked for messaging on my comni, but it wasn't working.

"Nope, that won't work here. Wait to sync with the Birch's system first," the Marthian pointed out. He was bothering me. "Are all the Marthians this annoying?" I wondered.

It didn't matter, he vanished from my sight and memory as soon as my foot walked through to the Main Base. On the left and right were very tall stewards that looked like they were at least three levels high. The stewards looked out of place in their bright blue suits. They were giant rock formations that moved and spoke slowly. Their translators knew every language in every galaxy, and they talked verrrry sloooowly.

My mom showed my ticket to one of the Birch stewards. They punched a hole into it, then synced my Comni with their communication messaging system. When that was complete, he bent forward, and a gap opened up where a large drone whirred out, followed by a four-wheeled cart to carry my cubes.

We looked left, right, and up and down like we had watched people doing earlier and followed the cart quickly, afraid of getting lost. The drone beeped, and the cart stopped. We stopped as well since the walkway had ended. The drone landed and chirped a few more times. A platform extended out in front of us, and a thick glass wall extended upward with railings. We stood on it-and the cart rolled on and whirled upwards. A voice announced, "This is Pod 33701," and we stepped off. The cart rolled into a large hallway. My comni beeped, and the door slid open.

FREE! STUFF

THE GREAT-GALACTIC

DANCE COMPETITION

VIP BOOK CLUB

✔ Parent Resources. Colouring Sheets, Crosswords, Puzzles.
✔ Bonus Scenes. Extra scenes not found in any books.
✔ Advanced Previews. Even new material before release!

www.kblaceyauthor.com

K.B. Lacey is a Canadian author. She lives just outside of Toronto, Ontario, Canada with her husband and two children who are the celebrities behind her stories.

Tryout is her debut Middle School Children's book.

For bulk orders or to book for pr engagements, Karen may be contacted through her website.

www.kblaceyauthor.com

Made in the USA
Las Vegas, NV
20 October 2023

79410070R00105